*That's a Good Question!*

# That's a Good Question!

## Expository Sermons on Crucial Biblical Questions

Tom Carter

**BAKER BOOK HOUSE**
Grand Rapids, Michigan 49516

# Contents

# Foreword

In *That's A Good Question!* Tom Carter presents a clear, concise series of messages that expound the riches of Jesus Christ. This book challenges the reader to live and share his or her life in Christ.

Using prominent biblical questions as his starting point, Pastor Carter blends practical illustrations, descriptive outlines, and personal applications to catch and keep one's attention right through to the final challenge of personal commitment to the Lord Jesus Christ.

These usable sermons were originally preached in the author's local church and broadcast on radio KRDU in Dinuba, California. I am pleased that they will now receive a worldwide reading. This book will be helpful to pastors in search of fresh sermon material and individual Christians who desire a closer walk with Christ.

David L. Hofer

Past President, National Religious Broadcasters

# Preface

*No man becomes a fool
until he stops asking questions.*

So said Charles Steinmetz, the brilliant German-born American electrical engineer.

People love to ask and answer questions. Television quiz programs prove that. But most of the questions on TV are trivial, such as, "How many state capitals border the Missouri River?" Other questions people ask can be embarrassing ("How old are you?"), impertinent ("Is that a toupee you're wearing?"), intrusive ("May I offer you some advice?"), or foolish ("Mom, do I have to go to school?").

The Bible, however, asks good questions—questions that deal with sin, salvation, knowing God, loving Christ, and serving people. But more than that, Scripture provides divinely inspired answers that, if followed, cause our lives to count for all eternity.

As a pastor I wanted the people in my congregation to think in terms of these crucial questions. So I pointed to fifteen that appear in the Word of God. The result was the series of sermons included in this volume. Each biblical

9

question has a purpose all its own—to instruct, comfort, challenge, encourage, pierce your heart with conviction, or save you from eternal death.

Many who heard these messages in our church experienced a reawakening to the essential matters of life. I trust that other preachers will find these sermons profitable toward that same end.

Tom Carter

# 1

# A Question of Salvation

"What must I do to be saved?" (Acts 16:30)

There are many good questions we need to ask ourselves throughout life. Children wonder, "What should I be when I grow up?" Later people ask themselves, "Should I pursue a college degree or join the work force after high school?" "Should I get married, and if so, to whom?" "Where should we live?" "How many children should we have?"

These are all good and necessary questions. We could add many more. But perhaps life's greatest question is the one asked by a first-century jailer in the city of Philippi. Acts 16:30 quotes him as saying this: "What must I do to be saved?" This is the most crucial question for all of us, because our response to its answer determines our destiny.

## The Crucial Question

Notice eight characteristics of this question.

### It Is Popular

In one way or another, everyone is asking the jailer's question. We all want wholeness, which is what salvation brings. Pagan savages have burned their children alive, hoping that such sacrifices will win the favor of their gods. People who experiment with sex and drugs search for peace, fulfillment, and joy down the road of pleasure. They long to be saved from their emptiness and despair.

Some people even punish themselves with guilt, hoping that self-imposed scourges on their consciences will atone for their sins. Others suppose that if they attend church, teach a Bible class, contribute money to the offering plate, or serve on a church committee, the Lord will accept them. They gladly inconvenience themselves to do whatever it takes to become children of God. I think this is one reason cults flourish. They tell people how to be saved in simplistic terms they can be proud of. The gospel, on the other hand, humbles us with its teaching of salvation by the grace of God.

### It Is Providential

The Lord had prepared the jailer's heart by sending an earthquake to shake the foundations of the prison, break the doors off their hinges, and snap the chains from the prisoners' hands and feet. When the guard awoke, he assumed the men had escaped. With a distorted sense of honor he drew his sword and was about to commit suicide. The apostle Paul, who was one of the prisoners, cried out that no one had escaped and so saved the jailer's life.

Today God uses similar acts of providence to make us

think about eternal issues. It can be the loss of a job, a pro-
longed illness, a serious accident, or the death of a family
member that first directs a person's heart to Christ. God has
his ways of getting our attention.

In 1916, four years after the *Titanic* went down, a young
Scotsman stood up in a meeting in Hamilton, Ontario, and
testified as follows:

"I am a survivor of the *Titanic*. When I was drifting alone
on a plank that awful night, the tide brought Mr. John Harper of Glasgow, who was also on a piece of wreck, near me.

"'Man,' he said, 'are you a Christian?'

"'No,' I answered, 'I am not.'

"He replied, 'Believe on the Lord Jesus Christ, and you
will be saved.'

"The waves bore him away, but strange to say, brought
him back a little later. Again he asked me, 'Are you a
Christian now?'

"'No,' I answered, 'I cannot honestly say that I am.'

"He repeated, 'Believe on the Lord Jesus Christ, and you
will be saved.'

"Shortly after that he went down. And there alone in the
night, with two miles of water under me, I believed that Jesus
Christ paid for my sins. I am John Harper's last convert."

What circumstance is rocking the foundations of your
life today? Whatever it is, don't let it go for nothing. Use
your trials to drive you to Christ and his forgiving love.
God works in unusual ways to lead us to faith in his son.
And the Philippian jailer would testify that even the most
painful methods are worthwhile.

### It Is Polite

After the earthquake struck that night in Philippi, the
jailer could have rushed over to the missionaries and

screamed, "Why have you caused me so much trouble? You brought your religion in here and it has cost me my prison, my job, and almost my life. If that's what Christianity produces, I want no part of it."

But he said no such thing. It's wonderful how God's process changes a person's attitude. Instead of resentment there was reverence in the jailer's heart. A few hours earlier he had thrown the missionaries into prison (v. 24). Now he rushed in trembling and fell down before them.

How is your attitude toward spiritual matters? Maybe you chuckled under your breath when you read the title of this sermon, as if it were unrelated to your life. But the jailer of Philippi was earnest when he asked, "What must I do to be saved?" All of us would do well to follow his example and take this question seriously. It could mean the difference between heaven and hell.

### It Is Passionate

The twenty-ninth verse reports that the jailer "called for lights and rushed in and, trembling with fear, he fell down before Paul and Silas." He was in anguish over his spiritual condition, and the missionaries honored his desperate desire to get right with God. Paul and Silas did not reply, "Wait until you cool off, and then see if you still want to be saved. You're in no emotional condition to make such a decision now. You shouldn't commit yourself to anything while in the heat of passion." Instead they immediately responded to his need. When the jailer's heart went out to God, the hearts of God's men went out to him.

### It Is Pressing

Here was a man who had to know right then and there how to be saved from his sins. Even though it was midnight, he could not sleep until he discovered the answer to his question.

Yet many people today are content to allow years to pass without giving their hearts to Jesus. They intend to do it someday, but it can wait. If you are not right with God don't go to bed tonight until you have settled this. Don't go anywhere until you have turned yourself over to Jesus, sins and all.

When Aaron Burr was a young man he attended a revival meeting at Yale University. During the sermon he was under deep conviction of heart. When the speaker gave a public invitation to receive Christ, Burr started to walk forward. Then he heard someone whisper in a mocking tone, "Look at Aaron Burr! He's going to the counseling room!" Embarrassed, Burr returned to his seat, replying to the critic, "Don't get excited. I was only fooling."

In later years he shot and killed Alexander Hamilton and was accused of treason and bartering America for his own gain. How different he would have been if he had not put off making his commitment to Christ! Just as salvation was a pressing matter for the Philippian jailer, so it is for each one of us.

### It Is Personal

Notice that the guard asked, "What must *I* do to be saved?" This man was not particularly evil. He was an officer of the peace, a civil servant. He was not part of the mob that opposed Paul and Silas. He did not know that the missionaries were innocent. Sure, he imprisoned Paul and Silas, but he was only following orders. People respected this man and felt safe with him on the job. He illustrates the truth that even moral, decent people need to know Christ personally.

Many a Christian wife would humble herself and receive Jesus for her husband if she could, but it doesn't work that way. Christian parents would pay any price to have their rebellious children surrender to the Lord. But those wayward sons and daughters must personally accept Christ. Until each person says, "Yes, salvation is something *I* want," he or she cannot be part of God's family.

### It Is Practical

The jailer could have said, "I hear you two men are Christian teachers. Can you tell me how a fish could swallow Jonah? And do you really believe that God parted the Red Sea? And what about the doctrine of predestination? How do you harmonize that with human responsibility?"

Instead of those theological questions, he asked a practical one. He wanted to know how to become new. Perhaps the area of theology that most puzzles modern people is the presence of evil in our world. They wonder how to reconcile it with a God of love. A person makes theology personal and practical by confessing that his or her own heart is filled with evil and then seeking deliverance from it through faith in Christ.

### It Is Primary

Nothing is more important than salvation. We don't find the jailer asking, "What must I do to receive a raise in salary?" or, "What must I do to get my temper under control?" or even, "What must I do to enjoy a better relationship with my wife?" Those questions have their place. But this man put first things first when he asked, "What must I do to be saved?"

Are your priorities in order? Too many of us major in minors and minor in majors. One thing that always seems to put my priorities back in place is a funeral. When I conduct one, I see people whose hearts are grieving, who would give anything to have their loved one back. This is especially true when the deceased person is a non-Christian. At such times all my problems, dreams, and plans pale into insignificance. I am reminded that what really matters in life is preparing to meet God. When we give primary things first place in our lives, our Lord takes care of the rest. As Jesus said in Matthew 6:33, "Seek first His kingdom and His righteousness; and all these things shall be added to you."

## The Authoritative Answer

In Acts 16:31 Paul and Silas reply to the jailer's question: "Believe in the Lord Jesus, and you shall be saved."

### It Is Simple

Paul and Silas did not load the man down with the spiritual baggage of rituals, ceremonies, or works to perform. They told him to do something simple: believe. The New Testament illustrates the simplicity of faith in several ways. Jesus compared it to taking a drink of water (John 4:14), sitting down to a free and sumptuous feast (Luke 14:16–17), accepting an invitation (Matt. 11:28), walking through a door (John 10:9), and letting someone in through a door (Rev. 3:20). His parable of the prodigal son teaches us that receiving new life is as simple as coming home (Luke 15:11–32). According to Paul, salvation is as easy as receiving a gift (Rom. 6:23), entrusting a possession to a capable and faithful guard (2 Tim. 1:12), and taking a shower (Titus 3:5).

In short, finding new life in Christ is as easy as believing. A Moslem, if asked the question, "What must I do to be saved?" might answer, "Repeat the words, 'There is no God but Allah, and Muhammad is his prophet.' Give money to beggars, keep the fasts, read the Koran, and make a pilgrimage to Mecca."

I have been told that a Hindu priest would say, "Observe the rules of the caste. Worship the monkey and the cow. Crawl on the ground to the sacred temple and try to please the many divinities."

The Buddhist, on occasion, has answered: "Forget about your body. Give no thought to pleasure or pain. Strive to attain Nirvana, the blessedness of extinguished passions."

The adherent of Confucius might reply, "Study the teachings of Confucius and learn the rules of righteousness. You will then learn the path of duty and of saving yourself."

But the Christian's answer to life's greatest question is outstanding for its simplicity. "Trust in the crucified Christ to rescue you from the penalty your sins deserve."

The gospel is so simple many cannot accept it. Remember Naaman? Elisha told him he would be cleansed from his leprosy if he would dip himself in the Jordan River seven times. But that was too elementary for Naaman. He expected something more painstaking, more complex. If his servants had not persuaded him to obey Elisha's order, he would have returned to his native Syria a doomed man.

Many people still reject the gospel merely because it's easy. If God told us to receive forty lashes across our backs, we would line up to do it. If he required us to perform manual labor for twenty years, we would work hard to be saved, because we could preserve our pride. But when we learn that eternal life comes through simple faith in Christ, we say, "There must be something more to it than that." After pondering this for years I am convinced that God insists we exercise simple faith in Christ so that Jesus can receive all the credit. The only real difficulty is overcoming our own pride. The simplicity of the gospel works humility in us.

## *It Is Sure*

Paul and Silas did not answer the jailer, "Believe in the Lord Jesus, and maybe, perhaps, quite possibly you'll be saved." No, they gave a definite answer: "You shall be saved." They were certain that if this man exercised faith in Christ he would become brand-new.

Would you like to have a salvation you can be sure of? Don't let your enormous sins cause you to doubt God's promise. He knows your sins better than you do, yet he still invites you to receive new life. There is no doubt in my mind that if you ask Jesus to give you a new heart, he will. His honor and integrity depend on it.

## Personal Application

I see a solemn contrast implied in this text: If you do not believe in the Lord Jesus, you will never be saved any other way. Putting off this all-important decision never settles anything. Your sin problem will not solve itself. Refusing to trust Christ does not bring peace. Relationships with people other than Jesus can bring you happiness but not the wholeness for which God created you. Neither can your work, education, or pleasures.

The opposite of salvation is condemnation. Both are easy to acquire. Salvation comes through simple faith in Christ, and condemnation is the result of simple neglect of him as one's personal Savior from sin.

In one way or another everyone asks life's greatest question: "What must I do to be saved?"

Now that you know the answer, what will your response be?

# 2

# A Question of Profit

"What will a man be profited, if he gains the whole world, and forfeits his soul?" (Matt. 16:26).

$M$ost people enjoy a good bargain. You and I know men and women who cannot resist a garage sale when they see one. They have to stop the car and inspect all the secondhand merchandise. Sometimes they arrive home with a carload of great purchases, much to the chagrin of their spouses.

And then there are people who are always talking about the stock market or their latest investments. To hear some of them you would think life is nothing more than a never-ending war against inflation. They are always trying to stay on top.

And look who's talking! Many of my friends consider me the kingpin of the bargain hunters.

Our Lord appeals to our sense of economy, our concern for profit and loss, when he asks the following good questions in Matthew 16:26: "For what will a man be profited, if he gains the whole world, and forfeits his soul? Or what will a man give in exchange for his soul?"

## The Possibility of a Lost Soul

Jesus mentions the case of a man who loses his soul. I believe we should take that very seriously as something that could happen to us. Just the sight of a lost dog evokes our pity. The news of a lost child in the mountains breaks our hearts. When we hear of an airplane that becomes lost to radar contact, we send out search planes and helicopters. Then we wait on pins and needles, praying there will be survivors.

I once heard Paul Harvey on his national radio program tell of a young man who had lost his doctoral dissertation just a few days before he would have turned it in. It represented four years of research, and Paul Harvey asked the people of America to report to him if someone found it so he could return it to the owner.

These losses are tragic. But not as tragic as a lost soul. A lost soul is simply someone who does not know Jesus Christ as his or her personal Savior. I can think of four characteristics that describe such a person.

### You Are Deserted

If you are apart from Christ you are utterly alone. You may think you have plenty of company and that you can all face God together. But on the judgment day you will have no one to defend you when you answer for your sins. Anyone who might have argued your case will be standing in line for judgment himself. You, therefore, will be totally deserted.

Thomas Paine wrote *The Age of Reason*, declaring that people should cast aside their superstitious belief in God. But on his deathbed he cried out, "O Lord, help me! O Christ, help me. Stay with me. It is hell to be left alone."

The French atheist Voltaire uttered these frightening words just before he died: "I am abandoned by God and man. I shall go to hell. O Christ, O Jesus Christ!"

These men were lost souls who knew they were deserted. You may be a lost person and not know it. But you, too, will eventually be abandoned by God and man if you remain in that condition.

### You Are Defenseless

A lost soul is someone who is defenseless against ultimate condemnation. There is nothing he can do to save himself. He can strive to please God by attending church, giving his money to Christian causes, being a model spouse, and performing a host of other good works. But all the effort in the world to earn membership in God's family is futile. The best thing a lost person can do is plead guilty, confess his sins, humble himself before God, and pray for God's grace to rescue him from eternal loss.

### You Are Desperate

If you are now living without Christ you are in the process of perishing. First Corinthians 1:18 speaks of those who "are perishing" (note the present tense). I cannot think of a more desperate condition than that of a person who is on his way to hell. He is like a man trying to swim against a current that is too strong for him and will soon wash him down a waterfall he cannot possibly survive. I believe the old saying, "Where there's life there's hope." But when a nonbeliever dies, all hope vanishes forever. From that point on his eternal destiny is fixed.

### You Are Doomed

Scripture speaks of a lake of fire in which people are tormented forever. It describes hell as a place of outer darkness where men weep and gnash their teeth and where the devouring worm never dies.

As a psychology major in college I visited a mental hospital. I shall never forget the hopeless groans and constant shrieks of terror in that depressing place. I remember thinking, "This is what hell is going to be like." And yet I am sure the wailing of the damned is far more terrifying than that.

Maybe you think I am appealing to your emotions to try to win you to Christ. I admit that, and I am not ashamed to do it. Hell *is* real. Many people *are* lost. But now let me shift gears and appeal to your business sense of profit and loss.

## The Profit of a Lost Soul

Look at our text again. Jesus says, "What will a man be profited, if he gains the whole world, and forfeits his soul?" In 1 John 2:16 we gain insight into the meaning of that phrase, the whole world. It defines "all that is in the world" as "the lust of the flesh, and the lust of the eyes and the boastful pride of life." Let's imagine that you could fully indulge in each of these three areas of worldliness.

### The Lust of the Flesh

This is the desire to do something God has not allowed. Maybe you have always had a secret wish to cruise around the world, live in a posh home, or spend all day in front of a TV set. Sounds harmless enough. But let's suppose that in your case these desires represent a preoccupation with pleasure.

When I was nine years old my parents had a tennis court built in our backyard. For me it was love at first sight. Throughout the summer I was practicing or playing from dawn until dusk. During the school year I retreated to my personal paradise virtually every afternoon, luring friends with the baits of fun and competition. I resented rainy days and lived for the crisp sound of a tennis ball volleying off my catgut strings. Of course, there is nothing sinful about tennis, but I think my indulgence exceeded God's allowable balance for my life. Hours spent on the court interfered even with my quiet times with God and thus became a symptom of the lust of the flesh.

### *The Lust of the Eyes*

Think of this as the desire to have something God has not given. In modern language it is called window shopping. We walk downtown, look in the store windows, and say, "I'd like one of those, two of those, and a half dozen of those." That's a subtle way to give free reign to the lust of the eyes.

One Christmas morning in my childhood my parents gave me a beautiful three-speed bicycle. Proudly I pedaled it to a friend's house, expecting him to be impressed. But he had just received a ten-speed bike that was fancier, faster, and more expensive than my three-speed. I immediately craved it. That morning the lust of my eyes stole the joy of receiving exactly what I had wanted for Christmas.

On August 1, 1990, Iraqi President Saddam Hussein ful-filled the lust of his eyes by sending his army to invade and seize the oil-rich country of Kuwait. The entire world was outraged and imposed international sanctions on Iraq. It could not export its oil or import sufficient food staples. U.S. President George Bush sent countless tanks, ships, jets, and military personnel to the Persian Gulf in preparation for imminent war with Iraq. Even the Soviet Union teamed up with the United States against Saddam Hussein. But the Iraqi dictator refused to back down. His craving to possess what his eyes lusted after rendered him incapable of withdrawing his troops from Kuwait, a country twenty-one times smaller than his own.

Now suppose Saddam Hussein could own *all* the countries of the world. Or assume you could possess everything you have ever laid your eyes on—all the expensive clothes, sports cars, homes, swimming pools, businesses, jewelry, and money you could desire. Even that would only be a third of all the world has to offer in exchange for your soul.

### The Boastful Pride of Life

This is the desire to be something God has not willed. What if you could be the world's most famous and well-loved celebrity? Or the best-dressed man or woman in the world? Or the president of the United States? Or anything else you've ever wanted to be?

Now put all three of these categories together. What if your every urge to *do* something, *have* something, and *be* something could be fulfilled? Then you would have gained the whole world. But even all of that, if bought at the price of your soul, would be a bad deal. What would your profit be? "Not a thing," Jesus says. Worse than that, it would be a total loss.

Yet countless people sell their souls for a lot less than this. Take Judas, for example. He cashed in to Satan for thirty pieces of silver. You may be willing to sell out for the price of one pornographic magazine, one adulterous affair, or a job promotion that requires you to sacrifice your Christian ethics. These things are infinitesimal in propor-

tion to the whole world. Yet gaining even that would be no
bargain at the expense of your right standing with God.

Throughout history many people have tried to gain the
world. Alexander the Great set out to accomplish this in
the fourth century B.C. He conquered all the then-known
world, and after that he mourned that there were no more
worlds to conquer. He proved that worldliness really does
not satisfy the human heart. King Solomon of Israel gained
virtually the entire world, having become proverbially the
wisest and wealthiest man in history. But even he con-
cluded, "Vanity of vanities! All is vanity!" (Eccles. 1:2).

Charlemagne reigned as emperor of the Holy Roman
Empire from A.D. 800 to 814. When his tomb was discovered in Aix-la-Chapelle, royal robes hung loosely on his
skeleton that sat on a marble throne with a crown still resting on his skull. Quite significantly, someone had placed a
Bible in Charlemagne's lap and pointed his bony finger to
our text: "What will a man be profited, if he gains the
whole world, and forfeits his soul?"

And let's not forget Satan. He's "the god of this world" (2
Cor. 4:4). But would you be willing to forfeit your soul in
exchange for the service of countless people?

The asking price for the world is just too high. This old
hymn is correct:

> If I gained the world but lost the Savior,
> Were my life worth living for a day?
> Could my yearning heart find rest and comfort
> In the things that soon must pass away?
> If I gained the world but lost the Savior,
> Would my gain be worth the life-long strife?
> Are all earthly pleasures worth comparing
> For a moment with a Christ-filled life?
>
> —Anna Olander

No! It would be no gain, no bargain, no profit to sell out to the world at the price of our salvation. We forfeit the world, anyway, when we die. And for many of us that will be soon.

## The Pricelessness of a Lost Soul

In the second half of our text, Jesus asks, "Or what will a man give in exchange for his soul?" Here is a picture of a man who sells his soul to gain the world, then discovers he made a bad deal. What now can he give to buy his soul back? Nothing.

If you make a bad exchange in business, you can usually recover it if you're willing to take a loss. If you sell a car for five thousand dollars, then regret letting it go, you might be able to buy it back for ten thousand dollars. You take a loss, but at least you get your car back.

But if you sell your soul, you cannot redeem it. Nothing can make up for this tragic loss, because your soul is priceless, and you have nothing else of equal worth. Not even the whole world can redeem a lost soul.

### The Savior's Crucifixion Proves This

If there had been any other way for the heavenly Father to ransom our souls except through the death of his Son, he would surely have chosen that way. If God could have purchased us out of sin with silver and gold, he would have done it. He owns all the wealth in the world, but even that could not buy us back from sin. Why? Because we are priceless.

There was, however, one other priceless thing in the universe—Christ's blood. Do you want to know how precious you are? Precious enough for the Son of God to leave his heavenly throne and stoop all the way to Bethlehem's manger. Precious enough for Jesus to spill his blood on a criminal's cross. Precious enough for him to endure God's wrath for you. Only that offering would suffice when it came to rescuing your lost soul and mine.

### The Sinner's Condemnation Proves This

Have you ever thought that endless punishment in hell was too stiff a penalty for a lifetime of sin? Have you ever wondered why God doesn't punish someone with seventy years in hell for seventy years of rebellion on earth?

The reason hell lasts forever is that lost people have sold a priceless soul. No amount of time can compensate for its loss. When Jesus asks, "What will a man give in exchange for his soul?" we feel like answering, "How about ten thousand years of suffering in the fires of hell? Surely that would be sufficient." But it isn't. Nothing is.

A man begins to sell out when his attitude, in effect, is, "I'd rather have the world than Jesus. I don't need a Savior from sin. I prefer to live for my career rather than for Christ. I choose to find my joy in money rather than in the Master. I'm going to pursue my goals rather than the glory of God." This man could be moral, a loving family man, and a respected leader in his community. But he has left Jesus Christ out of his life. If he dies without repenting of that attitude and lifestyle, he sells his soul irretrievably.

## Personal Application

Now a parting word to two groups of people. First, to the Christian. Since souls are that valuable, shouldn't we be more eager to win them to Christ? We parents are concerned that our children are well fed, well dressed, and well educated. Fine. But, mom, how valuable is your son's soul to you? Dad, how much time do you invest teaching your daughter about Jesus Christ?

And what about the people all around us? Are we going

to stand idly by while they perish? If they insist on going to hell, at least we should require them to burst through the barriers of our prayers, love, and verbal witness of Christ. It does not matter if we are criticized, slandered, or despised. What does matter is that people made in God's image are heading for a Christless eternity. I call persecution a small price to pay if only some of them will listen to our warnings and turn to our Lord. We sing this in an old gospel hymn:

> Give me a passion for souls, dear Lord,
> A passion to save the lost;
> O that Your love were by all adored,
> And welcomed at any cost!
>
> —Author unknown

Now to the non-Christian I must say that if you should die today, you would be eternally lost. But it doesn't have to be that way. It pays to give your life to Christ. It's the greatest bargain you will ever receive, for God adopts you as his child, forgives your sins, and gives you eternal life—all in exchange for faith in Christ. The best way to make sure you don't forfeit your soul is to give it to Jesus for safekeeping.

Will you do that now? "For what will a man be profited, if he gains the whole world, and forfeits his soul?" Nothing.

But what will a man be profited, if he gives his heart, soul, and life to Jesus Christ? Everything.

So then, whisper this prayer to God, in the words of Frances Havergal:

> Take my love, my God, I pour
> At Thy feet its treasure store;
> Take myself and I will be
> Ever, only, all for Thee.

# 3

# A Question of Love

"Do you love me?" (John 21:15–17)

Du) uring the Second World War, General Dwight Eisenhower corrected another general for referring to a soldier as "just a private." He reminded him that the army could function better without its generals than without its foot soldiers. "If this war is won," he said, "it will be won by the privates."

In the same way the everyday Christian is the backbone of the church. We have famous evangelists and dynamic pastors. But shepherds don't reproduce sheep; sheep do. And if the gospel is going to reach the lost, then for the most part, the ordinary Christians must take it to them. If you are a believer, you are a servant of God. You may not know it. You may not act like it. You may not be living for the Lord. But Jesus has called you to a life of service.

"So where do I begin?" you ask.

John 21:15–17 answers that question. It reveals the one crucial ingredient that Christ requires in all his servants.

## The Condition for Service

Three times, once in each of these verses in John 21, Jesus commissioned Peter to service. But first he asked him, "Do you love Me?" More than anything else Christ wanted *love* from Peter. Without that the apostle would have been unfit for ministry. And still today, before we can serve Christ, we must love him.

The story begins in verse 15: "So when they had finished breakfast, Jesus said to Simon Peter, 'Simon, son of John, do you love Me more than these?'" There are three different ways we can interpret the phrase *more than these*. Perhaps Jesus was saying, "Do you love me more than you love these other disciples? Am I more dear to you than your closest friends or family?"

Can you say you love the Lord more than anyone else on earth? Perhaps as a parent you have idolized your children. Or maybe you have resented God for allowing a family member to die prematurely. These are just a few telltale signs of our loving people more than Christ.

Jesus is impressing Peter with a preeminent claim on his love. And he demands our foremost love as well. More than anyone else he deserves our love, because he sacrificed himself on the cross for us. As he said in John 15:13, "Greater love has no one than this, that one lay down his life for his friends."

The second possible understanding of these words is this: "Do you love me more than you love these fishing boats and nets?" In the context of this verse, Peter had just abandoned his fishing boat in the sea, and with a flush of enthusiasm he swam ashore to meet Jesus. So our Lord could be saying, "Are you truly more devoted to me than you are to your work, or was your so-called demonstration of love merely an impulsive act?"

To us Jesus might put it this way: "Is your attendance in church a genuine mark of love and worship? Or is your mind even then on your job, your career, or your golf game? Does your devotion to these things betray a lack of love for me?" Cecil Frances Alexander had this idea in mind when she wrote in her hymn:

> Jesus calls us; from the worship
> Of the vain world's golden shore,
> From each idol that would keep us,
> Saying, "Christian, love Me more!"
>
> In our joys and in our sorrows,
> Days of toil, and hours of ease,
> Still He calls, in cares and pleasures,
> "Christian, love Me more than these!"
>
> —Cecil Alexander, 1852

Or third, maybe Jesus' words *more than these* mean, "Peter, do you love me more than these other disciples love me, as you once bragged that you did?" This would take us back to the night of our Lord's arrest. Shortly before Peter denied his master, he boasted, "Even though all may fall away because of You, I will never fall away" (Matt. 26:33). The Amplified Bible, Good News Bible, and the Good-speed, Weymouth, and Moffatt versions all translate John 21:15 in this sense, with some such rendering as, "Do you love me more than these others do?"

Peter replied to Jesus, "Yes, Lord; You know that I love

You" (John 21:15). In the original Greek language, Peter changed the term Jesus used for love. Jesus employed the word *agapao*, which is the purest and highest kind of love. Its noun form is used in John 3:16, which describes God's redeeming love for a sinful world, and nine times in the great love chapter of the Bible, 1 Corinthians 13. But when Peter answered, "I love You," he used the Greek word *phileo*, which speaks more of warm affection than pure, holy love. We can hear this nuance in the Living Bible, among others, where Peter responded, "You know I am Your friend." Obviously the apostle had been humbled by his denial of Christ. He was no longer making wild claims of his infinite love for his Lord.

I think it is also significant that Peter said nothing about the other disciples. He had once bragged that his devotion to Christ was superior to theirs. But here he answered for himself alone. We do well to follow his example and look only at ourselves when we evaluate our love. We do not excuse ourselves by saying, "Jesus, I confess that I'm not sure about my love for you. But look at John over there. He lies, cheats, steals, and neglects you. So at least I'm closer to you than he is." That's an echo of the hypocritical Pharisee's prayer that Jesus warned us about (Luke 18:9–14).

And isn't it interesting that Peter appealed to Christ's own knowledge in his answer? He said, "You know that I love You." And he repeated the words *You know* in all three of his replies. Experience had taught Peter not to trust himself, so he submitted his love to the master's omniscience.

But Jesus wasn't through with his disciple. "He said to him again a second time, 'Simon, son of John, do you love Me?' He said to Him, 'Yes, Lord; You know that I love You'" (John 21:16). This time our Lord dropped the phrase *more than these*, but he still questioned Peter's love. Again he used the word for holy love, *agapao,* and Peter answered by saying literally, "I am your friend."

Even a double emphasis on the question wasn't enough, however, for Christ asked him the same thing again: "He said to him the third time, 'Simon, son of John, do you love Me?' Peter was grieved because He said to him the third time, 'Do you love Me?'" (v. 17).

Perhaps Jesus' threefold question implies that love for Christ is the first, second, and third condition for our service to him. More than anything else, Jesus wants to know: Do we love him? His second most important concern is: Do we love him? And the third most important matter to him is: Do we love him? We might even say that's *all* he cares about, for he asked no other questions of Peter.

Isn't it significant that Jesus did not say, "Peter, will you *serve* Me?" Willingness is not the requirement for service; love for Christ is. Anyone who loves Jesus will not hesitate to work for him. Also notice that Jesus did not ask, "Peter, are you *sorry* that you denied me?" There's no rebuke here, no rubbing salt into the wound. Nor did Jesus inquire, "Do you love my *Word?*" or "Do you love my *church?*" These things would follow if Peter loved Christ.

I am sure Jesus did not enjoy grieving Peter. But even if it meant pain for his closest disciple, the master had to know the answer. Maybe this question makes you uncomfortable, too. But since Jesus died on a cross to prove his love for us, we should be able to examine our hearts. I fear that people who cannot face this question are headed for something much worse than an uneasy feeling. Love for Christ is not only the prerequisite for service but also the evidence of salvation. This is why Jesus declared that the foremost commandment is that we love him with all our heart, all our soul, all our mind, and all our strength (Mark 12:29–30). Nothing is more important than that.

In the first two questions Jesus used the term *agapao*, suggesting pure and holy love. Peter responded with the word *phileo*, meaning friendship. But on the third inquiry Jesus borrowed Peter's word. The Living Bible captures the sense with its paraphrase, "Are you even my friend?" Most commentators say that Peter was grieved because Jesus' threefold question reminded him of his threefold denial. No doubt that's true. But I believe the apostle's conscience was also pricked because Christ challenged even his claim to friendship. Again from the Living Bible, John 21:17 says, "Peter was grieved at the way Jesus asked the question this third time."

Peter replied, "Lord, You know all things; You know that I love You" (v. 17). He was saying, "You know that I'm your friend. I can't say my love is all it should be, but I do love you as a friend."

Do you love the Lord Jesus, even if not in the deepest spiritual sense? You may hesitate to answer, uncertain of your feelings. That reminds me of a story from Peter Marshall's life. A young man who was contemplating marriage asked him, "How do you know when you're in love?"

Marshall was quick to reply, "Brother, when you're in love, you'll know!"

Are you certain of your love for Christ? You may answer, "Of course I'm in love with Jesus. Don't my good works prove it?" No, they don't. Christ is not asking about your conduct; he is inquiring about the condition of your heart. You may be a Sunday school teacher, a deacon, a choir member, an usher, or someone serving Christ outside the church. I am a pastor, but that does not excuse me from asking myself, "Do I love my Lord?" Everyone must probe his own heart for the answer to this crucial question. Jesus insists on finding out.

That is the condition for service to Christ. Sometimes before a church will assign a ministry to someone, he must join the membership or sign a statement of faith or pass a test or agree to a code of ethics. But those things are incidental to Jesus. All he cares about is our *love*. If we can truly say, "Yes Lord, you know that I love you," he is ready to commission us to his work. Peter had fulfilled the condition for service. Have you?

## The Commission to Service

Just as Jesus' question and Peter's answer were voiced three times, Jesus also commissioned Peter three times. The first is found at the end of verse 15: "He said to him, 'Tend My lambs.'" Here, again, the master did not ask, "Do you love lambs?" The lambs represent young Christians who may be immature and weak. Jesus' point is that even if some of them rub us the wrong way, we will still serve them out of love for him. Anyone involved in ministry is sure to meet people who are hard to get along with. But our impetus for continued service must not be their lovableness but Christ's. In our ministry to them we minister to him.

Tending Christ's lambs refers mainly to feeding them, and for Christian lambs it is best that we dish out the milk and meat of God's Word. Peter himself wrote years later: "Like newborn babes, long for the pure milk of the word, that by it you may grow in respect to salvation" (1 Peter 2:2).

That's a good reminder to us servants, because a consistent diet of scriptural teaching is out of vogue in many churches today. Instead, leaders spend their time entertaining the lambs, tickling the lambs' ears, or even allowing the lambs to graze wherever they want and eat any blade of false teaching that may look attractive. But we must labor to feed the lambs the body-building nutrients of God's Word.

The second part of the commission, which differs slightly from the first, is seen at the end of John 21:16: "He said to him, 'Shepherd My sheep.'" Now the lambs have grown into sheep. This is part of the discipleship process, helping new Christians become strong saints. But it does not end here, because even full-grown sheep require shepherding. This activity speaks of protecting, nurturing, leading, and caring for the sheep.

Sheep are prone to wander and therefore need constant guidance. Matthew 9:36 tells us that Jesus was filled with compassion for people, because they were like sheep without a shepherd. That is why he calls on us to shepherd others in the faith. It is the crying need of every sheep.

The beautiful thing about this commission is that Jesus invites us to share in his own great work. He called himself "the good shepherd" (John 10:11). And years later Peter referred to Christ as "the Chief Shepherd" (1 Peter 5:4). Before God allowed Moses to lead the nation of Israel he required him to tend sheep in the desert for forty years. The greatest king of Israel, David, was chosen by God while he was still a shepherd. This is how authentic leaders are made, and in some way every servant of Christ ought to be in a shepherding ministry. Even if it is to no more than our own children, we should be shepherding or nurturing them toward maturity in Christ.

The end of John 21:17 gives us the third and final part of the commission: "Jesus said to him, 'Tend My sheep.'" The triple emphasis that Jesus placed on tending lambs or sheep stresses the need for this kind of servant. Deep down inside you and I want to be useful to our Lord. We long to be worthy shepherds and feeders of the lambs. And Christ will trust us with that ministry—if we love him.

We feel overcome with awe that Christ will put us to work even if we cannot profess to have the purest love for him. Peter could only say, "I am your friend," but that was enough for Jesus. He knew it would blossom into *agape* love. So let's not wait until we are super saints before we enlist in our Lord's task force. There is work to do now. No matter at what point you are on the road to sanctification, be encouraged, for Peter himself was once a backslider, and Jesus restored him.

## Personal Application

The stress our Lord placed on this question, "Do you love Me?" suggests the intensity of his love for us. It also shows that love can be absent even from an apostle's heart; therefore, we cannot assume we have fulfilled the one condition for Christian service. We must continually ask ourselves, "Do I love Christ?"

Many people have a zeal to know when Jesus will return. Others want to know his will for their lives. Still others yearn to know the contents of Scripture. Nothing is wrong with these quests for knowledge. But far more important than any of them is the assurance that we *love* Christ. Even if examining our hearts causes us, like Peter, to squirm, when we come to the point where we can sincerely answer, "Lord, You know that I love You!" joy will wash away all our discomfort.

Love for Christ will make our trials easier, strengthen us against temptation, inspire in us courage to witness to nonbelievers, prevent us from laying up our treasures on earth, and cause us to look forward to our arrival in heaven. In short, love for our Lord will equip us to be servants he can use.

But what if you cannot honestly say you love Jesus, even as a friend? Then go back to Calvary. Watch the Savior bleed and die on a criminal's cross in your place. Understand that his greatest suffering consisted of his bearing the world's sins in his body. Nothing creates the fires of love in a cold human heart like a look of faith to the crucified Christ. When you come back from Calvary you will be able to say as never before, "Lord, You know all things; You know that I love You!"

# 4

## A Question of Lordship

"Why do you call Me, 'Lord, Lord,'
and do not do what I say?" (Luke 6:46)

Carl F. H. Henry is one of the twentieth
century's leading evangelical theologians. At the conclusion
of an interview conducted by *Discipleship Journal* he was
asked, "What do you look forward to God doing with the
rest of your life?"

Dr. Henry answered, "I just want to be obedient. I don't
think God asks success of any of us. He gives it when it
pleases him. And the person who has been obedient and
whose life is a failure, as humans look at it, is as successful
as the most successful saint in the history of the Church"
(19, Jan. 1, 1984, p. 15).

In Luke 6:46–49 Jesus uses a parable about tragedy to

awaken us to the truth that the proof of his lordship of our lives is not our willingness to listen to his words—whether that be seen in church attendance, an interest in Bible study, or a fascination with sermons. Instead, *the foundation of an authentic Christian life is obedience to Jesus' commands.*

## A Challenge

In Luke 6:46 Christ asks this challenging question of his disciples: "Why do you call Me, 'Lord, Lord,' and do not do what I say?" A lord is a master, someone who deserves unconditional obedience. But when we rebel against, or even neglect Jesus' commands, we invalidate our testimony to the world that he is our Lord. If we are disobedient in our Christian practice, we are dishonest in our Christian profession.

A fourteen-year-old boy saw in a shop window a sign that advertised, "Boy Wanted." He presented himself for work inside. The storekeeper took one look at him and figured he wasn't old enough to be employed, but he asked him, "Well, young man, what can you do?"

"I can do what I'm told, sir," the boy answered.

That so pleased the shopkeeper that he said, "You'll do, my boy, you'll do!"

Christ is looking for people who will do what he tells them. "If you can't obey me," he says, "then don't call me 'Lord.'"

God ordered Joshua to lead the Israelites in a march around the city of Jericho for seven days and then shout its walls down. Surely some of the people, on hearing that, raised objections. I can see them coming forward with their own ideas of how to conquer Jericho. No doubt Joshua himself had a standard military strategy in mind. But he

turned a deaf ear to the voices all around him that told him
God's way would never work, he put aside his own plans,
and he obeyed his Lord. That was his secret of victory over
the city of Jericho.

Obeying God's commands is also our secret of victory
over sin and Satan. Bear in mind that we are talking about
obedience to the *Lord,* not to the *law.* This is submission to
a person, not a set of rules. That makes it satisfying.

Years ago, while visiting my parents at their home, I
noticed that a bird had built its nest in a flower pot my
mother had hung from the ceiling of the back patio. When
I showed the nest to her, she asked me to lift it out and
move it to a corner of the patio. But the bird abandoned it
and built a second nest in that same flower pot. We felt
sorry for all the extra work we had caused our feathered
friend, so we left her nest alone.

We often treat Christ as my mother and I treated that
bird. He comes into the center of our plans and interrupts
them. We feel inconvenienced, so we bump him off center
stage. Though we call him Lord, we make liars of ourselves
by trying to move his carefully built "nest" away from that
special place and into some corner of our lives where it
won't be noticed. But Jesus persists in doing the same thing
in the same place. And when we continue to resist him we
wonder why our lives are full of problems. Quite simply,
we didn't obey.

Many of us are like the woman who said:

> I didn't have potatoes,
> So I substituted rice.
> I didn't have paprika,
> So I used another spice.
> I didn't have tomato sauce,
> I used tomato paste—

> Not half a can, a whole can—
> I don't believe in waste.
> A friend gave me a recipe,
> She said you couldn't beat it.
> There must be something wrong with me;
> I couldn't even eat it!

No wonder her dish was inedible. She didn't use any item the recipe called for. And how often have we made substitutions in God's recipe for our lives? Maybe you substituted a non-Christian mate for a believing one. Perhaps the Holy Spirit has entrusted you with the gift of evangelism; but instead of using it to win people to Christ you are dedicating it to your career as a salesman. Such disobedience puts us to shame when we call Jesus our Lord.

## A Contrast

In verses 47–49 we have a contrast between two people. One listens to the words of Christ and follows through with obedience. The other merely listens.

### The Person Who Acts on Christ's Words

In the forty-seventh verse Jesus says, "Everyone who comes to Me, and hears My words, and acts upon them, I will show you whom he is like." Notice three characteristics of this person.

First, *he is deep in his trust*. Jesus says "he is like a man building a house, who dug deep and laid a foundation upon the rock" (v. 48). Elsewhere Scripture says "the rock was Christ" (1 Cor. 10:4). Edward Mote understood this in his hymn:

> On Christ, the solid rock, I stand,
> All other ground is sinking sand.

Our text describes someone who digs deeply into the soil of God's Word and fixes his faith on the rock of Jesus Christ. His trust in the Lord is not superficial; his spiritual roots are deep.

But what is the evidence of this? His obedience. That is the litmus test of faith, because Christ often asks us to do what looks foolish in the eyes of the world. Are you willing to act on the Word of God, even if others mock you for it? When Abraham obeyed the divine command to lay his son Isaac on the altar of sacrifice, he probably feared that his wife would unleash her wrath on him and his friends would write him off as a lunatic. But God had spoken, and Abraham was willing to trust him with the consequences of his obedience.

A pilot was having difficulty landing his plane because of the fog, so the control tower decided to bring him in by radar. While the pilot was listening to the directions he remembered a tall pole in the flight path. Quickly, and in a state of panic, he screamed, "Please let me change my course! I might hit that pole!" But the tower replied, "You obey instructions; we'll take care of obstructions."

The person who is deep in his trust will obey the Lord's instructions and rely on him to take care of obstructions.

The second thing about the obedient hearer of Christ is that *he is durable through his trials.* Jesus goes on to say, "When a flood rose, the torrent burst against that house and could not shake it" (v. 48). The flood symbolizes times of overwhelming grief, loss, tribulations, and personal afflictions. Even the obedient servant of God can expect the hour of crisis to flood into his life. No one is immune from the severest of trials. So don't be caught off guard when they surge into your experience.

The good news is that the person who puts his faith into

action will remain stable through his trials. If we have built our lives on the rock of Christ through personal obedience, the crisis will threaten but will not destroy us. Jesus is saying, "Obey me, and your life will weather the storm." We don't want a fair-weather faith that only sees us through when circumstances are kind. We need an anchor that will keep us stable through the storm, and that anchor is Jesus. But more than that, the chain that ties us to the anchor is our obedience to his words.

Christ says the storm couldn't even shake this man's house, much less destroy it. I've seen this in many believers' lives. A woman is rejected by her friends or her husband because of her faith in Christ. Such rejection would be intolerable to someone else, but this woman is not shaken. Why? Because she has already put her hand to the plow and is not looking back, as the one she calls Lord demanded. She cannot be shaken. A man is dying of a terminal disease, wasting away outwardly. But inwardly he is being renewed day by day. Why? Because years earlier he took up his cross in obedience to his Lord. Even in death he cannot be shaken. Isn't this the kind of endurance we all look for when the torrents of trouble crash against the homes of our hearts?

A third mark of the obedient disciple is that *he is defended against his temptations.* Jesus says the house could not be shaken "because it had been well built" (v. 48). The river bursting against the house is an illustration not only of trials but also of temptations that threaten the spiritual life. The well-built defense against these satanic assaults is a faith that obeys.

Everyone is building a life. In Jesus' parable both the obedient and the disobedient men constructed a house. The difference is that only the person who acted on Christ's words had a life that was built well enough to defy the onslaught.

What about your life? Are you an easy mark for any luring bait the enemy might place in front of you? Sometimes we offer the excuse that we are no match for the devil. But when the foundation of our lives is settled on Christ through a faith that obeys, we can withstand even Satan! That's not my statement, but Jesus'.

### The Person Who Merely Hears Christ's Words

Now Jesus describes the man whose life is not well built. He listens to the commands of Jesus but does not carry them out. He claims that Christ is his Lord, but his disobedience says otherwise. He sings, "Fairest Lord Jesus," but desires worldly trinkets ahead of Jesus. He recites, "The Lord is my shepherd," but lives as if Christ were a thief who is out to rob him of happiness. Verse 49 tells us three things about this person who is willing to listen to Jesus but fails to obey him.

First, *he is detached from Christ.* The master says, "But the one who has heard, and has not acted accordingly, is like a man who built a house upon the ground without any foundation." Doubtless this man believed in foundations, but he thought one was unnecessary for his house. He was eager to start building right away, so he took a shortcut and skipped the digging. Though his home looked normal, in reality it was as flimsy as a house of cards.

He represents people who attend church, listen to the sermon, hear the Bible read, even say they believe it all, and then do nothing about it. They have Christian beliefs but not Christian behavior. They gain outward respectability as religious people—the houses of their lives look just like the houses that are built on the rock—but they have no deeper, hidden experience. They do not dig into God's Word. They do not invest time in the inner room for prayer. And they do not yield themselves to the indwelling power of the Holy Spirit. They may argue about religion, even give their testimonies, but they fail to live what they say they believe.

Could this be you? Don't apply this verse to someone who despises Christ, for Jesus is talking about people who eagerly listen to him. Maybe you have been building your life on the sand of pleasure, education, money, or success. Perhaps you have come to Christ for what you can get out of him. Fine—but don't stop there! The stable foundation in this parable is not what we can get out of Jesus but what he can get out of us, namely, our obedience.

Our society is sick because it has not dug deeply enough. We call ourselves a Christian nation, yet abortion is legal and homosexuality is regarded as an acceptable alternative lifestyle. Our national motto is "In God we trust," but in fact we trust in wealth and power and worldliness. We give superficial lip service to Jesus when we should render him solid life service. Unless our faith results in obedience, the house of our lives is not on the rock; we are detached from Christ.

The second thing about this listener is that *he is defenseless without Christ.* This happened to the house of his life: "The torrent burst against it and immediately it collapsed, and the ruin of that house was great" (v. 49). As in the case of the obedient man, the river bursting against this house represents the various trials of life, including temptations. Our Lord says that the second house collapsed immediately. It had no stability at all. If our faith is only on the surface, evidenced by our lack of obedience, we will easily be blown away by difficulties.

I am sure we should also see in the river bursting against

the house a reference to the final judgment. This most clearly explains "the ruin of that house was great." It was great because a precious person created in the image of God slipped into eternity apart from Christ.

Merely saying that Jesus is our Lord will not get us into heaven. Elsewhere he warns that not everyone who calls him Lord will enter the kingdom (Matt. 7:21). We only prove the genuineness of our faith when we put Christ's words into practice. And if we don't we will be totally defenseless and entirely without excuse on the judgment day. Eternity will then echo this sad verdict: "The ruin of that life was great."

Finally, this can be said about the person who listens to Jesus, calls him Lord, but does not obey him: *He is deceived about Christ.* We read this caution in James 1:22: "But prove yourselves doers of the word, and not merely hearers who delude themselves." What do mere hearers of Christ delude themselves about? Their relationship to him. In the end they discover that they are not his disciples after all, and he is not their Lord.

## Personal Application

The most hardened atheist I know is a man who exposes himself to some of the finest evangelists and pastors in the world. He loves to watch preachers on television. He understands the gospel but he thinks it all nonsense. There are others who for years have faithfully attended the church in which I preach, but they, too, are lost. Sometimes I feel like asking them, "How many sermons will it take before you submit to Christ? Five thousand? Ten thousand?"

Here in Luke 6:46–49 Jesus has taught us that hearing his truth is not the dividing line between children of God and children of the devil. A faith that obeys is. So practice some frank evaluation before God. Ask yourself, "Am I an obedient disciple, or just a deluded listener? Do I possess spiritual depth, or am I superficial? Does my faith in Christ stand on a solid foundation, or on a rotten trap door? Do I make complete work of repentance from sin, love for Christ, and service to him, or have I opted for the short-cuts? Has Jesus enabled me to withstand the storms of life, or do I only possess a fair-weather faith? When I call Christ 'Lord,' does my behavior confirm my claim?"

You really have not grappled with this portion of Scripture until you have confronted yourself with questions like these.

But a final caution is in order. It would be wrong to rush out in a flurry of activity, desperate to do everything possible to obey God in an attempt to earn your salvation. That is the error of salvation by works. Jesus is talking about the obedience of *faith*. When your faith says, "Love compels me to obey the Christ who died for me at Calvary; my heart's desire is to glorify him," you have begun to dig deeply. And it will not be long before you find the solid rock.

# 5

# A Question of Indifference

"Is it nothing to all you?" (Lam. 1:12)

In the nineteenth century Henry Drummond wrote a classic little book titled *The Greatest Thing in the World.* It is all about love based on 1 Corinthians 13:13, which says: "Now abide faith, hope, love, these three; but the greatest of these is love." Jesus said the two most important commandments are those that tell us to love God and our neighbor (Mark 12:29–31). And the apostle Paul told the Galatians that "the whole Law is fulfilled in one word . . . love" (Gal. 5:14).

If love is the greatest virtue we can practice, it stands to reason that the worst sin must be the opposite of love. Is

51

that hatred? Not really. As bad as hatred is, at least it takes the other person into consideration. The opposite of love is something much more cold and pale than the burning zeal of hatred. It is *indifference*.

Lamentations 1:12 is about indifference. The verse is in the context of Jerusalem's downfall in 586 B.C. King Nebuchadnezzar and his Babylonian army had just pillaged the once beautiful city with its glorious temple. Jeremiah lived to see that day, and with poetic license he allowed Jerusalem to speak for itself in the words of Lamentations 1:12:

> Is it nothing to all you who pass this way?
> Look and see if there is any pain like my pain
> Which was severely dealt out to me,
> Which the LORD inflicted on the day of His fierce
>     anger.

Jerusalem seems to say, "Does no one care that God's holy city and its people have been conquered by the heathen?" But no one did care.

### Indifference Toward the Lost

Now I want to take these words out of the mouth of the holy city and put them on the lips of others. First, I believe we can take this question as coming from people who do not know Christ and are therefore perishing. I realize that many of them have felt no need for salvation. But if they only understood their lost condition they would cry out to us who have found the way and say, "Is it nothing to you that I am perishing? Can you just stand there and watch me go to hell?"

### Their Condition without Christ

The Bible describes the condition of a non-Christian in alarming terms. He is dead in sins (Eph. 2:1), as well as separated from Christ, a stranger to God's promises, without hope, and without God in the world (Eph. 2:12). He has been spiritually blinded by Satan (2 Cor. 4:4). His mind is hostile to God (Rom. 8:7). And not only is he *in* the dark, but is darkness itself (Eph. 5:8). All of this and more is included in the statement that the nonbeliever is spiritually lost.

These are people you and I know: a family member, a neighbor, a friend from work or school. Think of that person now, then imagine a voice coming from his soul, which is created in God's image. That voice says to you and me, "Is it nothing to you that I am in this condition? Don't you care that I'm lost?"

These people sense that something is wrong. That's why they search for wholeness in illicit sexual relationships, drugs, alcohol, and a host of other worldly gods. You and I know they will only discover fulfillment in Jesus Christ. How, then, can we be indifferent to their condition?

### Their Conduct against Christ

Look around and see the damage that a lost person wreaks on this world. Does it break your heart when you notice pornographic magazines in grocery and convenience stores? Do you care that homosexuality is regarded today as an acceptable alternative lifestyle? Does it make you grieve when people take the life of an unborn child as if he or she were nothing more than a piece of tissue? With the current AIDS epidemic, we might expect people to repent and turn to God. But instead our society talks about how to have "safe sex." Can we who believe in a holy God remain nonchalant when men and women are disregarding him?

A tragic case of spiritual indifference occurred when Pope Gregory X in A.D. 1271 received a letter from Kublai Khan, the Mongol emperor in China. It read, "You shall go to your high priest, Jesus Christ, and pray on our behalf to send me one hundred men skilled in your religion. And so I shall be baptized, all my barons and great men shall receive baptism, then their subjects will be baptized, and there will be more Christians here than in your parts."

What an opportunity for evangelism! But Pope Gregory X never replied to the letter. If he had not been indifferent, if he had commissioned missionaries to China with the gospel of Christ, the entire spiritual climate of the east might be drastically different today. But all we can say now is, "If only. . . ."

### Their Contempt of Christ

When Jesus died on the cross, the religious leaders mocked him with such words as, "He saved others, but he can't save himself!" And ever since he has been disdained by many in the unbelieving world. Some think of him as an effeminate nobody who is totally irrelevant to modern life. They consider it beneath their dignity to worship him, an act of intellectual suicide to trust him, and a Sunday school fantasy to speak of a Savior from sin.

Is it nothing to us that people have such contempt for our Lord who died for them? How can we be insensitive to the scorn that nailed Christ to his cross? Shouldn't the world's contempt of Jesus stimulate us to work for their conversion? Can we stand by and do nothing when our Lord is despised?

### Their Condemnation from Christ

Sometimes we shrink from thinking about eternal punishment in hell. But the reality remains. If we Christians don't explain to perishing people the way of salvation, no one else will. The gospel is their only hope of heaven. There was a time when just the thought of hell would make us tremble. But now many of us could stand at the mouth of the bottomless pit, hear the cries of the lost, and not feel so much as a pang of pity.

Read again our text from Lamentations 1:12 and see if it could also be the cry that ascends out of the awful abyss:

> Is it nothing to all you who pass this way?
> Look and see if there is any pain like my pain
> Which was severely dealt out to me,
> Which the LORD inflicted on the day of His fierce anger.

"I believe that if there is one thing that pierces the Master's heart with unutterable grief," wrote F. B. Meyer, "it is not the world's iniquity, but the church's indifference." That convicts me. Too many times my own heart has been lukewarm or even cold when it should have been white hot to win the lost.

Some years ago I told a Christian friend that I knew an elderly man who needed Christ. I said I was planning to visit him. A few weeks passed, and my friend asked me if I had seen the man. I answered no. He asked me how old he was, and I said "eighty-seven."

Then my friend jolted me out of my sinful indifference by saying, "If that man is lost, he has only a brief time before he will be in hell. Don't you think you should visit him right away?"

Aware that his eternal destiny was hanging in the balance, I went that afternoon and lovingly urged him to invite Christ into his heart. I had been awakened to the need. And that's what I'm praying God will do to you today.

## Indifference toward the Lord

Now I want to shift gears and apply this text to Jesus Christ. I can hear him say, "Is it nothing to you that I suffered the greatest sorrow and pain anyone has experienced, all for your sake?" Let me show you how our Lord's suffering was unique in several ways.

### His Unique Person

It was the sinless Son of God who died at Calvary in our place. And yet millions of people couldn't care less. It's nothing to them that so great a person died for them.

John Griffith worked as a controller of a railroad bridge spanning the Mississippi River. On a daily schedule he raised the bridge so that ships could make their way down the Mississippi, then lowered it so that freight and passenger trains could rush across. In the summer of 1937 John Griffith took his eight-year-old son Greg with him to work for the first time. He showed little Greg the control house where he operated the bridge. At noon he and his son shared lunch on the observation deck.

Then John returned to the control house to close the bridge, leaving Greg on the observation deck. As he glanced down under the bridge to see if any ships were under it, he saw something that made his heart leap into his throat. Greg had slipped from the observation deck and fallen into the gears that operated the bridge.

John was faced with a crisis decision. If he pulled the lever, his son would be crushed to death among tons of steel. If he did nothing, he could save little Greg, but a train full of people would die. At the last second he made his decision. He pulled the lever. The gears turned, the bridge came down, and his son was killed.

As the train roared across the bridge, John lifted his face, now smeared with tears, and looked into the passing windows of the train. Businessmen were reading their newspapers. Women were chatting or reading to their children.

In soul-stirring agony John Griffith cried out to the train, "I sacrificed my son for you! Don't you care?"

But nobody heard him, and the train rushed by.

I believe God is saying to us, "I sacrificed my Son for you! Is it nothing to all you who pass by?"

Are we listening? Can you hear the Lord speaking?

### His Unique Proxy

Jesus was the only person in the universe who could have taken our place on the cross, because he alone was God and man at the same time. More than that, he was the only one who *did* die for us. But do we care?

On January 13, 1982 Air Florida flight 90 took off from National Airport in Washington, D.C. Moments later it crashed into the Fourteenth Street Bridge. Many died, but some survivors were rescued from the icy waters of the Potomac River. As the helicopter lowered the rope down to the survivors, one man kept giving it to others, who were then pulled to shore. The hero's name was Arland Williams. Five times they lowered the rope to him, and all five times he passed it to someone else. Finally he was the only one left to save. But when the helicopter returned, he had drowned.

Do you suppose his death meant anything to the five people whose lives he considered more important than his own? Merely to ask the question is to answer it. Why, then, is it nothing to so many that Jesus sacrificed himself for them?

Someone once said, "Jesus wept that he might one day wipe all tears from the eyes of millions. He sorrowed that multitudes might rejoice. He shed his blood that many a bleeding heart might be healed. He tasted death that a new life might be breathed into the souls of men."

Yet all of that is nothing to countless millions who pass by in this life. What a tragedy!

### His Unique Pain

An old hymn based on Lamentations 1:12 says:

> All you who pass by,
> To the Savior draw nigh;
> To you is it nothing that Jesus should die?
> For sins not his own He died to atone;
> Was pain or was sorrow like His ever known?

No! No pain, no sorrow has ever matched his. I suppose other people have endured as much physical agony as Jesus in his crucifixion. But no one has been tormented with equal spiritual suffering. Even people in hell are not afflicted as much as he was. They bear the consequences for *one* life of unbelief and sin. But God unleashed on Jesus the punishment meant for all the billions of people who have ever lived and ever will live.

Sometimes we get caught in the trap of thinking our pains are the worst the world has ever seen. It might be the loss of a job, a divorce, a huge financial debt, wayward children, or radical surgery followed by chemotherapy treatments. I don't want to belittle these problems, for they are unusual. But they are not unequaled. Others have walked through those same valleys. Jesus, however, can truly say, "There is no pain like my pain. His sufferings were unique.

### His Unique Price

First Peter 1:18, 19 reminds us that Christ did not redeem us with corruptible things like silver and gold. He bought us with his blood. Yet many people remain unmoved.

In the account in 2 Samuel 23, King David of Israel was hiding from the Philistines in the cave of Adullam. He thought back to his childhood days in Bethlehem and spoke longingly of the refreshing waters from the well in that city. Some of his mighty men broke through the enemy camp, drew water from that well, and brought it back to their king. But David could not drink it. Instead, he poured it out on the ground to the Lord. In 2 Samuel 23:17 he explained by saying, "Shall I drink the blood of the men who went in jeopardy of their lives?"

David was not indifferent to the danger his men had risked for him. Although they lost not a hair from their heads, David looked at that water and considered it their blood.

But Jesus did shed his blood. He did die. Yet, who cares? So few! It was something to David that his men had been willing to sacrifice their lives. But it is nothing to most people today that Jesus poured out his infinitely precious blood.

## Personal Application

Once more let me ask you this question: Is it nothing to you who pass by that Jesus suffered the most agonizing death the world has ever seen, to such an extent that his pains were unparalleled?

I trust that in your heart you answer, "Yes! It's something

to me that Jesus sacrificed himself for my sins. More than that, it's *everything* to me."

Then give Christ your heart. Trust him as your Lord. Live every day for his glory. Share his gospel with others who have never heard or are confused about it. Since Jesus died for you, be willing to lay down your life for him. Make Christ preeminent in everything you do.

As God's child commit yourself to prove to the world not only that Jesus is *something* to you but that he is *everything* to you.

# 6

# A Question of Belief

"Who has believed our message?" (Isa. 53:1)

Wouldn't it be frustrating if you discovered a cure for AIDS or cancer, and no one believed you? Imagine doctors scoffing at you and refusing to prescribe your drug for their patients. You walk down the hallways in hospitals, enter the rooms of the AIDS or cancer patients, and share with them the good news that if they only swallow the pill in your hand, they will recover. But they refuse to take it. Wouldn't you be burdened for them to believe and be healed?

That was similar to the concern the prophet Isaiah felt when he cried out in chapter 53, verse 1 of his book, "Who has believed our message? And to whom has the arm of the LORD been revealed?" In the New Testament sense we could

put it like this: "Who has accepted the good news of forgiveness, sonship to God, and eternal life through faith in
Jesus Christ? To whom has the Lord given new life?" Isaiah
couldn't point to one believer, and his lack of success in
ministry burdened him for the lost.

Are you burdened for the lost, or have you lost your
burden?

Isaiah's question is one that every Christian should have
on his heart. Every pastor and evangelist should pray after
every sermon, "Lord, who has believed our message?"
Perhaps not in those exact words, but they should represent the heartfelt attitude of every servant of God. We
should be eager to see people trust Christ for their salvation and every other need.

On May 10, 1891, Charles Spurgeon told his congregation at the Metropolitan Tabernacle in London, "If no soul
gets saved through this discourse, I cannot carry on my
business. . . . If my hearers are not converted, I have lost
my time; I have lost the exercise of brain and heart. I feel as
if I had lost my hope and lost my life, unless I find for my
Lord some of his blood-bought ones; and I must find some
of them by this sermon" (*Spurgeon at His Best,* Tom Carter,
ed. [Grand Rapids: Baker, 1988], p. 69).

John Knox prayed, "Lord, give me Scotland, or I die!"
John Welch testified, "I am out of breath pursuing souls."
When Hudson Taylor was a young man, he told God, "I
feel that I cannot go on living unless I do something for
China." In 1858 the other missionaries in Ningpo called
him a "poor, uneducated nobody." No mission would back
him, so he founded the China Inland Mission and went on
to become a pioneer of missions in China. His great influence even led to the establishment of many more faith missions. God honored his burden.

Henry Martyn, after landing in India, said, "Here I am in the midst of heathen midnight and savage oppression. Now, my dear Lord, let me burn out for Thee." In twelve short years his life was over, but his prayer was answered.

David Brainerd enjoyed an effective ministry among the North American Indians. His journal discloses his secret of success: "I cared not where or how I lived, or what hardships I went through, so that I could but gain souls for Christ. While I was asleep I dreamed of these things, and when I awoke the first thing I thought of was this great work. All my desire was for their conversion, and all my hope was in God."

Robert Arthington was not able to travel overseas, but he sacrificed to help others reach unbelievers. His apartment was a single room. He cooked his own small meals. He lived on a bare-bones budget that resulted in his giving of more than a half–million dollars to foreign missions. He wrote, "Gladly would I make the floor my bed, a box my chair, and another box my table, rather than let men perish for lack of the knowledge of Christ."

Are you burdened for the lost, or have you lost your burden?

Some Christians say it's God's job, not theirs, to win nonbelievers to Christ. Their responsibility, they claim, is merely to witness. Whereas there is some truth in that statement, it's incomplete. Can we be content merely to speak of Christ and not see anyone won to him? Not when we realize what's at stake.

Win Arn puts his finger on the problem when he writes this:

The biblical concept of "lostness" has disappeared from the conscience of most churches and most Christians. In our modern culture, the understanding of what was once a theological imperative—of people outside Christ being eternally lost—has changed in the minds of many believers. . . . Little remains of the first-century Christian's burning conviction that without Christ, every person is forever lost. Nor is there that fervent zeal for non-Christian friends and relatives which swept across America as great evangelists graphically portrayed the terrifying damnation of a God-less eternity (*Church Growth America*, Jan-Feb, 1982, p. 10).

What if Isaiah had said, "Lord, who cares if anyone has believed our message? So what if the arm of the Lord hasn't been revealed to anyone lately? At least I've done my part by preaching to this ungrateful bunch." The reason the prophet did not talk that way is that he cared not only about his own duty but also for his people's salvation and his Lord's glory.

God warned Isaiah when he called him to preach that the people of Israel would not believe. He predicted that their hearts would be insensitive to his message, their ears dull to hear it, and their eyes dim to see it (Isa. 6:10). Still the prophet was burdened with grief when they did not believe. Instead of smugly saying, "Well, this is what the Lord told me would happen," he cried out, "O Lord, who has believed our message?"

How about you? Are you burdened for the lost, or have you lost your burden?

The prophets Nahum, Habakkuk, and Malachi all introduce their messages to their people as a "burden." They were weighed down with the desire to see men and women turn to God.

Of course our Lord Jesus carried this burden also. He once looked over the holy city and lamented: "O Jerusalem,

Jerusalem, who kills the prophets and stones those who are sent to her! How often I wanted to gather your children together, the way a hen gathers her chicks under her wings, and you were unwilling" (Matt. 23:37). The unbelief of the Jewish people wounded Jesus more than anything else.

Even when the Roman soldiers were pounding spikes through our Lord's hands and feet, he had a greater pain in his heart. Instead of screaming, "Oh, how those nails hurt!" he cried out, "Father forgive them; for they do not know what they are doing" (Luke 23:34). To him death was worthwhile if only his murderers would believe. His joy of providing salvation for sinners more than compensated for the agony of the cross. Why? Because Jesus was burdened for the lost.

The apostle John applied Isaiah's soul-stirring question to Jesus. Listen to his words in John 12:37–38: "But though He [Christ] had performed so many signs before them, yet they were not believing in Him; that the word of Isaiah the prophet might be fulfilled, which he spoke, 'Lord, who has believed our report? And to whom has the arm of the Lord been revealed?'"

Christ shared Isaiah's anguish. Our Lord did not walk around saying, "I have good news for you. But if you don't want to believe it, that's your business." Far from it! He lived with a burdened heart and died of a broken one, because people would not believe in him and so help themselves to God's abundant life.

Do you have a burden for the lost, or have you lost your burden?

When the apostle Paul read Isaiah 53:1, he said to himself, "That's the same heartache I feel in my ministry." He wrote in Romans 10:16, "Lord, who has believed our report?"

You may be thinking, "But Paul was an effective evangelist. He won countless people to Christ. Why was he grieving as if no one had believed?" The reason is that no matter
how many people are saved, many more always need to be
brought in. Paul proves that no matter how successful we
may be in evangelism we should never cease to grieve over
those who say no to Christ.

In Romans 9:2–3 Paul testified: "I have great sorrow and
unceasing grief in my heart. For I could wish that I myself
were accursed, separated from Christ for the sake of my
brethren, my kinsmen according to the flesh." He was willing to be damned in hell, if only his fellow Jews would be
saved in heaven. For Paul, even the lake of fire would have
its consolation if he could look up and see people in
heaven who had formerly been far from the Savior.

In 1 Corinthians 9:22, 23 Paul gave the secret to his spiritual fruitfulness: "I have become all things to all men, that
I may by all means save some. And I do all things for the
sake of the gospel." The apostle's chief desire in life was to
bring people to salvation in Christ. He was an outstanding
teacher, a brilliant theologian, and a persuasive debater. But
he was always disappointed with anything short of seeing
men and women made new. Paul understood that people
cannot be educated out of hell. He believed that the only
hope for sinful man is to become born again. That is why
he labored to see people saved.

Take another text from Paul. In 2 Corinthians 5:20 he
wrote: "We beg you on behalf of Christ, be reconciled to
God." Here was a man who was not ashamed to beg. He
threw embarrassment to the winds when it came to getting
people right with God. He did not take the dignified
approach of offering the gospel and then leaving men and
women to make their own decisions. He was not afraid to

get emotional over the issue of salvation, because eternity was at stake.

I once heard a pastor preach the gospel then tell his listeners, "It's your privilege to accept or reject Christ. If you don't want to trust Jesus as your Savior and Lord, you don't have to." Without realizing it, he was encouraging them to disobey the heavenly Father's command to believe in his Son. If it's our privilege not to trust Christ, why does God punish people eternally in hell for their unbelief? I submit to you that anyone who tells unbelievers that they can take or leave God's offer of salvation and doesn't urge them to repent of their sins has lost his burden.

One Sunday night after a church service in which I had preached, a man invited me out for a bite to eat. In the restaurant I told him that I was sorrowing for several people I knew who had been in church that night, were non-Christians, and did not respond to the invitation to receive Christ. My friend told me I would make a poor farmer. His point was that, like a farmer, a pastor sows the gospel seed in people's hearts. And, like a farmer, a pastor must patiently wait for the crop to grow and bear fruit.

He had a point. We should patiently endure. But we must never fail to urge listeners to surrender to the Lord at once. The Bible knows of only one time to get right with God, and that is "today" (Heb. 3:13, 15; 4:7).

On another occasion I received a letter in the mail from one of our church members, a dear woman who had a deep love for Christ. She knew that I was grieved over the mere trickle of converts our church was producing. She encouraged me that my messages were building the believers in their faith and were not, therefore, useless if no one was born again through them. But I replied to her that I aim my sermons at both Christians and non-Christians. And if the lost don't trust Jesus after hearing me preach, I haven't reached my goal for them. Yes, I know that God is the one who converts. But he also breaks hard hearts by means of tender hearts.

Years ago I wasn't that concerned for people without Christ. But God created a burden of grief in my heart for those who are perishing, and I don't want to harden my heart again. I don't want you to harden yours, either. The Lord will use you if you let him reveal to you the horror of people made in his image who are en route to hell.

Do you feel a burden for the lost, or have you lost your burden? Do you care that millions of people don't trust the same Savior you do? Do you mourn when you discover that many consider the gospel not worth their hearing, much less their believing? Doesn't it break your heart when you see people who prefer the witchcraft of sin to the grace of God? Can you feel Isaiah's anguish when he said, "Lord, who has believed our message?" Are you burdened?

If not, why not? Jesus suffered for us. Can't we feel for him? He endured our hell. Can't we bear his burden? Doesn't it hurt to think that people will believe in almost anyone who comes along, but not in almighty God? Every day people all over America open their newspapers to read the advice of an astrologer or Ann Landers, as if such speak the only truth. But do you think those readers search the Scriptures half as seriously to learn God's will for their lives? I don't.

You and I know people who will stay up all night watching election returns on television. Others will sit for more than three hours in a football stadium without a moment's boredom. Still others will stare spellbound at a movie for several hours in a theater. They believe in those things. (I myself have done them all.) But who has believed the message of the gospel—that salvation from sin and the free gift of eternal life can be theirs through faith in Jesus Christ?

Yes, I know many people have. But walk downtown sometime late at night. Stand outside the bars and ask yourself as you watch the people walk in and stagger out, "Who has believed our message?" Drive through a theater parking lot where a lewd movie is playing. Think of all the lives represented by those empty cars. Then ask yourself, "Who has believed the gospel message?"

Moms, you labored nearly to the point of death when you brought your children into this world. Do you feel an ache in your hearts for them to be born again? Do you wrestle with God in prayer for your children's salvation? If the first birth took some determination, you can be sure the second one will.

You businessmen and women, does it cause you pain when you see your peers believing in success, financial prosperity, and power, but not in your Lord Jesus? Do you have a burden for the lost, or have you lost your burden?

I think every Christian either *has* a burden or *is* a burden. If we feel no concern to see others won to Christ, we slow down the cause of Jesus and hinder the kingdom's progress. If you are a complacent Christian, pray that God will give you a burden. That is a prayer request he will be only too happy to grant.

## Personal Application

One more time. Isaiah asked, "Lord, who has believed our message?" Have you believed it? Have you made Christ your Savior and Lord and vowed to serve him the rest of your life? If you have no burden for the lost, it may be because you are one of the lost.

Who has believed our message? Anyone who confesses his sins to God, trusts in the shed blood of the crucified Christ as the ransom price for his sins, and invites Jesus into his heart as his personal Savior. Have you done that? If not, will you do it now?

I can almost hear someone say, "Yes, I'll believe! I see that I am lost apart from Christ, and I'll place my faith in him as my Lord and Savior today."

Then welcome to the family of God. Come on over the line. Stop being among the lost who are a burden, and join the ranks of those who are burdened for the lost.

# 7

# A Question of Sides

"Who is on the Lord's side?" (Exod. 32:26)

It was a dark day in the history of the people of Israel. Their gross idolatry in the worship of a golden calf would be forever etched in the pages of Holy Scripture as a testimony against them. We read of the sinful nightmare in the thirty-second chapter of Exodus. Moses was late in returning from his encounter with God on Mount Sinai, and the people were growing restless. They finally gave up hope of their leader's return and commissioned his brother to construct an image of God for them to worship. Aaron consented and fashioned a golden calf out of ornaments belonging to the people.

Soon the camp was out of control. Idolatry led to gluttony, drunkenness, and immorality in a chain of events that shackled God's people in the grip of sin. Although Moses

71

was the meekest man on earth, when he saw the depraved behavior he shattered the tablets God had just entrusted to him. Then he stood at the gate of the camp and with a mighty shout interrupted the lewd frolic with the challenging question found in Exodus 32:26 (KJV): "Who is on the LORD'S side?" Only the tribe of Levi responded. But may their tribe increase today!

We need that same call to commitment, because our society is rife with modern forms of idolatry. Even people who profess to know Christ are worshiping money, houses, jobs, recreation, other people, and a host of other modern counterparts to the golden calf. Sometimes it's hard to differentiate between those who are on the Lord's side and those who are not.

## Remarks about Being on the Lord's Side

Now let's get specific about what it means to be on God's side.

### In Relation to Salvation

First, being for the Lord means we accept eternal life as a gift of God's grace and not an achievement of our works. To try to earn salvation is to fight against Jesus for the prize of glory. The crucifixion of Christ is the death blow to all our efforts to win our own righteousness. When we view the Savior dying on the cross, we discover that he had to do for us what we could never have done for ourselves: accomplish the work of salvation.

I know of a woman who pays a cleaning lady to get her house in order every Thursday. On Wednesdays the woman exhausts herself scrubbing floors, cleaning the windows, doing the laundry, and washing the dishes. A friend asked her why she goes to all that trouble since she hires a cleaning lady to do those jobs. "Oh," she replied, "I'd be embarrassed to death if she saw my home in such a mess!"

Many people assume they must "clean up their act" before they can ask Jesus into their hearts. But that idea comes from Satan's side. People who are on the Lord's side are willing to humble themselves and let Christ clean up the mess.

### In Relation to Scripture

Second, being on the Lord's side means we accept everything we read in the Bible as the truth. We are not free to pick and choose the verses we believe and those we reject. We are not editors of God's Word but students of it. We must place ourselves under the authority of all Scripture. To criticize it and accuse it of fallibility is to place ourselves on the devil's side.

I know a Sunday school teacher who told his class that the story of Herod murdering the infants in Bethlehem was fiction, because only one of the four Gospel writers (Matthew) reported it. But how many times does God have to say something in his Word before we believe it? I'd say that teacher has no right to lead a class in Christ's church, for he's on the wrong side!

For several years I was on a panel of pastors from different denominations in a world religions class at a local high school. The students questioned us about many doctrines and practices. One asked me if I believed that a person had to be baptized to go to heaven. I answered no, and supported my reasons from Scripture. Immediately another pastor disagreed with me on the grounds that the traditions of his church have taught for centuries that baptism is a condition for gaining eternal life. I replied that the Bible is more authoritative than any church's traditions, and if those traditions contradict Scripture they should be discarded.

Neither the other pastor nor I was willing to budge, and the outcome was that the students witnessed two pastors on opposite sides. I'm confident that I was on the Lord's side, not because my opinions are better than his (for they aren't), but because I appealed to Scripture, and all he could cite were man-made traditions. Yes, this question, "Who is on the Lord's side?" needs to be posed even to pastors.

### In Relation to Submission

Being on God's side implies more than just believing his Word. It includes obeying it. One of the songs Frank Sinatra made popular was "I Did It My Way." That's the theme song of our human nature, which doesn't want to obey God. We think we know better than he what is good for us. Our Lord has given us a mandate to spread the gospel throughout the world. But we shirk our responsibility and busy ourselves with less important or even meaningless matters. Jesus told us to forgive people who have offended us. But we nurse grudges and allow bitterness to grow in the soil of our hearts. The reason we find this such a struggle is that we have failed to submit to the authority of Christ. Consequently, our claim to be on the Lord's side rings hollow.

### In Relation to Sanctification

Siding with God also means we pursue holiness and refuse to swim with the tide of society's moral permissiveness. Our world regards the idea of sin as dinosauric. The trend these days is either to defy the ethics God has ordained in his Word or to label the old sins such as drunkenness, lying, theft, and sexual perversions as diseases, not willful acts of rebellion against a holy God.

In answer to a critic, Abraham Lincoln asked, "If you count a cow's tail as a leg, how many legs does it have?"

"Five," was the reply.

"No," Lincoln said. "Just calling a tail a leg doesn't make it a leg."

I think we make a similar mistake. We can call sin by some other name, but that doesn't change a thing. People who are on the Lord's side don't resort to manipulations of God's truth. If we are to follow Christ we must accept our responsibility to forsake sin and grow in holiness.

Historian Arnold Toynbee wrote: "Of the twenty-two civilizations that appeared in history, nineteen of them collapsed when they reached the moral condition the United States is in now." Yes, even our nation, "under God," is for the most part not on the Lord's side when it comes to holiness of life. That's why Moses' question needs to be echoed today.

## Reasons for Being on the Lord's Side

One good reason for being on the Lord's side is that there is only one other alternative—the devil's side. In Matthew 12:30 Jesus said, "He who is not with Me is against Me." Many people don't want to be Jesus' enemies, but they have no desire to be committed to him, either. The Lord, however, doesn't allow us the luxury of compromise.

In Matthew 7 Jesus paints a picture of our spiritual life in black and white. He says there are only two gates through which people pass: the narrow gate that leads to eternal life and the wide gate that leads to destruction. There are two ways: the hard way leading to heaven and the easy way leading to hell. There are just two kinds of trees, representing certain people's lives: the good and the bad. There are two types of fruit, symbolizing our lifestyles: the good and the rotten. Jesus mentions two kinds of people: the wise and the foolish. He speaks of two foundations on which to build your life: the rock and the sand. And finally, he describes the outcome of every life by means of two houses: the one that stood the test of the storm and the one that was demolished by the storm.

There's no such thing as neutrality when it comes to Jesus Christ. To use his own words, "No one can serve two masters" (Matt. 6:24), a good reason why we should be dedicated to him alone.

A second reason for being on the Lord's side is that he orders us to love him with all our heart, all our soul, all our mind, and all our strength. Jesus went so far as to say this is the foremost commandment (Mark 12:29-30). Siding with God is the first step in fulfilling the highest commandment.

Third, we should get on the Lord's side because he purchased us with his blood. The result is that we are not our own; God rightfully owns us (1 Cor. 6:19–20). The death of Christ compels us to serve him. He gave his all for us. Can we do the same for him?

Fourth, we should stand with the Lord because his side will eventually win the war against Satan's camp. Everyone wants to be a winner. But if we don't enlist on God's side now, there will come a day when we will wish we had.

A final reason for throwing in our lot with the Lord is that it will even serve our own self-interests. God created us to enjoy a personal relationship with him. To rebel against him, then, is to rebel against our purpose. Life makes sense only when we are in harmony with the heavenly Father.

## Requirements for Being on the Lord's Side

Perhaps you feel that you are not totally dedicated to the cause of Christ. Let me then mention a few things that are involved in siding with the Lord.

### A Confession of Sin

When Moses asked, "Who is on the LORD's side?" I think he meant, "Who is willing to confess his sin and show his repentance by returning to the Lord?" The tribe of Levi responded positively. Surely they did not cross the line as an expression of their innocence in the golden calf affair, because Aaron himself was a Levite, and he built the idol. No, they were making a confession of sin.

Why didn't the other eleven tribes of Israel do the same? There can be only one answer: They were unwilling to humble themselves. I can hear them attempting to justify their behavior with the excuse that Moses had been given up for dead. But that didn't wash with God.

Today we fine tune the craft of excuse-making. I've heard more than a few couples say, "We know we shouldn't be living together before marriage, but we can't afford to pay rent on two apartments." Underneath it all they are saying, "We can't afford not to live in sin." And that's the devil's lie. So we must give an honest confession if we are going to line up with the Lord.

### A Consecration to Service

After the Levites took their stand for God at this time, and perhaps because of it, God set them apart as servants in the tabernacle (Num. 1:47-53). We can say, therefore, that people who are on the Lord's side are meant to be his servants.

Ephesians 4:12 teaches that the responsibility for service or ministry belongs to all Christians, not just the pastors. What are you doing for your Lord? Of course God gives us many different spiritual gifts. But I'd like to suggest that every believer should be involved somehow in the work of evangelism. We should all have a part in bringing others into a personal relationship with Christ. Shepherds don't produce sheep; sheep do. And in God's family the sheep are the everyday Christians. Are you on the Lord's side? Then show it by helping to fulfill his Great Commission, which is to "go . . . and make disciples of all the nations" (Matt. 28:19).

### A Connection with Saints

When the Levites walked forward at Moses' invitation, they left behind some of their old friends and formed a new family of faith. And our spiritual family as Christians is composed only of people who are in the camp of Christ. The visible expression of that is the church. Yet many believers avoid it. Surely if our faith in Christ is strong enough to take us to heaven, it should be strong enough to take us to church as well.

Many times people have asked me, "Can I be a Christian without attending church?"

Yes, you can. But it's something like being a student without attending classes or a soldier who is absent without leave or an athlete without a team or a salesman without any customers.

Can you imagine one of the Levites answering Moses, "Count me in. I'm on the Lord's side, but I'm going to stay right where I am"? Moses didn't give anyone a chance to say that, because he followed up his challenge, "Who is on the LORD's side?" with a command: "Come to me!" And after the pattern of Moses, I say that if you consider yourself one of God's people, display it by joining in fellowship with others who are also on the Lord's side.

### A Conflict against Satan

The first assignment Moses gave the Levites after they united with him was to draw their swords and slay those who had refused to be on God's side. The tribe of Levi obeyed Moses, and three thousand men died by their hand that day.

Our conflict today is against Satan, not people. Paul wrote in 2 Corinthians 10:3-5 (RSV): "For though we live in the world we are not carrying on a worldly war, for the weapons of our warfare are not worldly but have divine power to destroy strongholds. We destroy arguments and every proud obstacle to the knowledge of God, and take every thought captive to obey Christ."

Early in my pastoral ministry the local Methodist church advertised in the newspaper that they would teach a series of messages against the false doctrines of the cults. A Mormon wrote to the editor his opinion that churches should not lash out against other groups but just quietly preach their own gospel. The writer accused the Methodists of an unChristian attitude and behavior.

But I disagree. I commend that church for attacking satanic error. Its members were doing their part to destroy the works of the devil—the very purpose for which Christ came to our planet, according to 1 John 3:8. That Methodist church was proving to be on the Lord's side.

## Personal Application

Are you on God's side? Maybe you are afraid to take a stand for Christ because so few do it. But when we place ourselves on the Lord's side, he puts himself on our side. And one person plus the Lord is always a majority.

I love the way Frances Havergal reechoed Moses' question from this text in her beautiful hymn. I pass it on to you as a final challenge:

Who is on the Lord's side? Who will serve the King?
Who will be His helpers, other lives to bring?

Who will leave the world's side? Who will face the foe?
Who is on the Lord's side? Who for Him will go?

By Thy call of mercy, by Thy grace divine,
We are on the Lord's side, Savior, we are Thine.

—Frances Havergal, 1877

May that be your song to Christ today.

# 8

## A Question of Revival

"Wilt Thou not Thyself revive us again?"
(Ps. 85:6)

In his book *The Revival We Need,* Oswald
Smith describes the Welsh people in 1904 as being far from
God. Church attendance was poor and sin was rampant.
Evan Roberts began holding services, and soon spiritual life
was flourishing. The worshipers had no hymnals, no choir,
no advertising, and no offerings. But Roberts conducted worship from 10 A.M. until midnight seven days a week. Theaters
were forced to close for lack of interest. Even the mules in
the coal mines could no longer understand their masters,
because for the first time they weren't swearing at them.
Twenty thousand people were converted in five weeks.

In 1835 Titus Coan landed on the shores of Hawaii to
preach the gospel. The people thirsted for God's Word to

such an extent that Coan often preached three times before breakfast. For two years a continuous camp meeting was held in which two-to-six thousand were always present, night or day. One church recorded 5,244 new members in one year and 1,705 baptisms on one Sunday. In those two years Titus Coan baptized 11,960 converts.

I witnessed God move in revival in the Spring of 1970. One morning we students at Seattle Pacific College made our way to the daily chapel service, little realizing what was in store. The usual half-hour, midmorning routine was transformed into a shower of blessing that lasted beyond midnight. Students waited in line to express their praise to God before the entire assembly. Sins were confessed. Reconciliation took place between feuding brothers and sisters. Our campus was not the same after that. And similar revivals broke out at other Christian colleges that same month: Asbury in Kentucky, Wheaton in Illinois, and Biola in California. The Holy Spirit unmistakably signed his autograph on these revivals.

In Psalm 85:6 we find this good question, expressed in a prayer: "Wilt Thou not Thyself revive us again, that Thy people may rejoice in Thee?"

The word *revival* comes from a Latin word meaning "to live again." Because non-Christians are "dead in trespasses and sins" (Eph. 2:1), they have never been made alive in the first place. We Christians are the ones who need to be revived. We tend to grow spiritually complacent. When we do experience renewal, nonbelievers will desire what we have and turn to Christ. Evangelism, an expression of the church, follows revival, an experience in the church.

Charles Finney compared revival to a harvest of wheat. If you plant the seed in fertile soil, water it, and give it sunshine, it will grow and bear fruit. You can count on it, even though it's very much of a miracle. And so with revival. If we fulfill the proper conditions, we can expect the Lord to reawaken us.

Yet God is obviously withholding this vital blessing from most of his church today. Why? I can think of seven reasons.

## Uncommitted Lives

Too many of us are playing at Christianity. British evangelist Henry Varley once told Dwight Moody, "The world has yet to see what God can do with *one* person totally committed to Jesus Christ."

Moody replied, "By the grace of God, *I'm* going to be that person!"

He then went on to become the nineteenth century's most famous evangelist. During a four-month preaching mission in London, over 2.5 million people attended his meetings. According to church historian Bruce L. Shelley, writing in *The New International Dictionary of the Christian Church* (J. D. Douglas, ed. [Grand Rapids: Zondervan, 1974], 675), in the course of his life Moody traveled more than one million miles and addressed more than 100 million people. God honored his 100 percent commitment to revival.

On November 2, 1856, Charles Spurgeon, a twenty-two-year-old pastor, told his congregation, "I have now concentrated all my prayers into one, that I may die to self and live wholly for Him." Spurgeon served as pastor in that same church until his death more than thirty-five years later and is acknowledged today as the "prince of preachers." Though he died a century ago, his ministry is still kindling the fires of revival today. Why? Because he was totally sold out to Christ.

It doesn't take much of a person to bring a revival; it takes *all* of him.

## Unbent Knees

In the Welsh revival of 1904 a man who visited the meetings stood up and said, "Friends, I have journeyed to Wales with the hope that I may glean your secret of revival."

Evan Roberts instantly jumped to his feet and replied, "Brother, there is no secret! 'Ask, and you shall receive.'" How little we pray! And when we do, we often sound more as though we are reading a grocery list than pleading with God. The French churchman Fenelon said, "Of all the duties prescribed by Christianity, none is more essential and yet more neglected than prayer."

I'm not talking about all-night prayer meetings, just simple pleas to God for revival. James 4:2 says, "You do not have, because you do not ask."

## Unread Bibles

Scripture tells us how the Lord works, and outlines his will for our lives. In the Word we find God's promises, one of which is revival. But ignorance of the Bible deprives us of spiritual renewal. It's not surprising that Claire Cox stated in her book *New Time Religion* that the Bible is the "unread best seller."

At the end of the nineteenth century two English archaeologists, B. P. Grenfell and A. S. Hunt, traveled to the Faiyum region of middle Egypt to look for treasure. They began to excavate at Tebtunis, hoping to discover valuable primitive art. Soon they unearthed what seemed to be an ancient cemetery. But the bodies were those of crocodiles, which the Egyptians regarded as sacred. The reptiles were stuffed with nothing more than waste paper. Yet the archaeologists had come upon genuine treasure, because the waste paper was papyrus that dated back to New Testament times. It provided many examples of biblical words used in their contemporary setting. This has proven invaluable for understanding terms that otherwise would have been vague in meaning.

Many of us treat our Bibles like embalmed crocodiles. We regard them as nothing more than old hide on the outside and ancient paper on the inside. But in fact they contain valuable treasure. And unless we treat Scripture in our daily experience as precious, we will never unlock the door to revival. As Robert Coleman writes, "Systems of thought which discredit the Holy Scripture never produce revival" (Robert E. Coleman, *Dry Bones Can Live Again*, [Old Tappan, NJ: Revell, 1969], p. 32).

## Unconfessed Sin

Psalm 66:18 warns, "If I regard wickedness in my heart, the Lord will not hear." And Isaiah 59:2 states that our sins have hidden God's face, so that he does not hear our prayers.

A woman admitted to her pastor that she had a problem with exaggeration. "Let's ask God to forgive you for the sin of lying," he suggested.

"Oh, no!" she replied, "I'm not a liar. I only exaggerate."

Her pastor then informed her that she'd never be right with God until she confessed her sin for what it really was.

We all are prone to be like that woman. We easily admit we make mistakes, but we attribute them to general weakness rather than sinful willfulness. We easily recite Romans 3:23: "All have sinned and fall short of the glory of God." But it's something else to confess, "I am a condemned, hell deserving sinner."

Even when we go that far, we can still hide from humility behind the facade of general confession. We can stand up and say, "I'm a great sinner," and yet continue to resist specific charges. If someone replies, "That's right; you're a liar, a thief, and a glutton," we deny it at once. And so we run for shelter under the general term *sinner,* not to make confession but to escape it.

But this will never do. God does not send his shower of revival blessing to people whose hearts are hardened against it.

The 1949 revival in New Hebrides (Pacific islands) illustrates this truth. A small group of fervent Christians made a covenant with God that they would wait on him in prayer until revival broke out. Months passed, and nothing happened. One night a young man rose from his knees and read Psalm 24:3–5: "Who may ascend into the hill of the LORD? And who may stand in His holy place? He who has clean hands and a pure heart. . . . He shall receive a blessing from the LORD."

He closed his Bible, looked at the other Christians on their knees, and said, "Brethren, it is just so much humbug to be waiting night after night, month after month, if we ourselves are not right with God. I must ask myself, 'Is *my* heart pure? Are *my* hands clean?'"

Challenged, the others fell to their knees in confession and commitment. That night revival came to their town. The entire community was visited by the power of the Holy Spirit, and within a few weeks the revival had swept across the island, gathering literally thousands of people into God's family.

## Unforgiving Spirits

Reconciliation between enemies is always one of the ingredients in true revival. Jesus declared that "if you forgive men for their transgressions, your heavenly Father will also forgive you. But if you do not forgive men, then your Father will not forgive your transgressions" (Matt. 6:14–15).

Many readers are troubled by those words, as if we could earn God's forgiveness by forgiving others. Jesus' meaning, however, is simply that God does nothing halfway. If we confess to him one sin while clinging to another, he will continue to work on us. Our unforgiving spirit is itself a sin, and it along with all our other iniquities must be confessed and surrendered. We are hypocrites to ask the heavenly Father for pardon while we are unwilling to pardon people who have offended us.

Maybe you have a long-standing feud with someone, and you'd sooner die than be reconciled to him or her. This bitterness may even be directed against your own husband or wife. But without a sincere spirit of forgiveness there will be no revival.

## Unpaid Tithes

In Malachi 3:10 we read: "'Bring the whole tithe into the storehouse, so that there may be food in My house, and test Me now in this,' says the LORD of hosts, 'if I will not open for you the windows of heaven, and pour out for you a blessing until it overflows.'"

The tithe is one-tenth of our income. Malachi's contemporaries were not giving it to God. As a result, the passage goes on to state, insects devoured and plagues destroyed the crops.

I believe the principle of Malachi 3:10 holds today. Just as God vowed to open the windows of heaven and pour out rain in Malachi's day, he will open the floodgates of heaven today and pour out his Spirit in revival on us. But we must first cheerfully return to him at least a tenth of our income. If we expect to receive all that God promises, we must first give all that he asks. Until we do, there will be no revival.

## Unbroken Hearts

Many Christians feel little or no anguish in their hearts over people who are heading for a Christless eternity. The apostle Paul testified in Romans 9:2–3: "I have great sorrow and unceasing grief in my heart. For I could wish that I myself were accursed, separated from Christ for the sake of my brethren." He had a broken heart for his fellow Jews who were rejecting Christ. He was even willing to go to hell for them, if only they would trust the Lord Jesus.

God doesn't ask us to go to hell to rescue the lost. Jesus already did that when he died at Calvary. But our heavenly Father does ask us to be willing to travel to the ends of the earth with his good news of salvation. Yet most of us are unwilling to walk across the street. Then we wonder why God withholds revival.

Perhaps Richard E. Kunert's poem, "You Forgot," will help stir us out of our sinful complacency:

> You lived next door to me for years,
> We shared our dreams, our joys, our tears.
> A friend to me you were, indeed,
> A friend who helped me in my need.
> My faith in you was strong and sure;
> We had such trust as should endure.
> No spats between us ever rose,
> Our friends were like, and so our foes.
>
> What sadness, then, my friend, to find
> That after all you weren't so kind.
> The day my life on earth did end
> I found you weren't a faithful friend.
> For all those years we spent on earth,
> You never talked of second birth.
> You never spoke of my lost soul
> And of the Christ who'd make me whole.

I plead today from hell's cruel fire
And tell you now my last desire.
You cannot do a thing for me,
No words today my bonds to free,
But do not err, my friend, again,
Do all you can for souls of men.
Plead with them now quite earnestly,
Lest they be cast in hell with me!

## Personal Application

Maybe you think, "It would be nice to have a revival, but the cost is just too high. I'm satisfied with things the way they are in my own spiritual life and in the church. Let's just keep it that way."

But revival is more than a luxury; it is our absolute need. Revival is the only hope for the survival of our nation. As Alan Redpath once said, "If God doesn't judge America for its sin, He will owe an apology to Sodom and Gomorrah!"

Unless we experience revival, our country will be brought to its end in judgment. Unless we have revival, hell will be gorged with men, women, boys, and girls whom you and I know and love. Unless revival comes, Christ's body, the church, will continue to be held in contempt by the unbelieving world. Without a revival God will not receive the glory he deserves in our world.

Will God revive us again?

That's a good question. He certainly wants to. But to a great extent the answer depends on us.

# 9

# A Question of Security

"If God is for us, who is against us?" (Rom. 8:31)

Readers of the Bible sometimes fall into one of two extreme positions. Some presume that because God is loving he will never judge them, even if they refuse to believe in Christ. Others fear that, in spite of their faith in the Lord Jesus, God is going to punish them. The truth is that unbelief will condemn the best of us, and simple faith will save the worst of us.

In Romans 8:31 the apostle Paul addresses people who suffer from the second imbalance, people who fear that in spite of their standing in Christ the heavenly Father may still allow them to perish. To such believers he poses this question: "If God is for us, who is against us?"

Answers immediately come to mind. The devil is against us. The world is against us. Even our own human nature is against us, because it makes us vulnerable to sin. Granted, these are formidable foes. But Paul's point is that if God is on our side, we possess a strength that renders all our enemies powerless.

The New Testament clearly teaches that God is for the Christian. A husband is on the side of his wife, since they are one flesh. Good parents love and support their children, since they are part of the family. And in the same way our heavenly Father is on our side. He always has our best interests in mind. Verse 32 illustrates how far God went to prove he is for us. He "did not spare His own Son, but delivered Him up for us all."

During the First World War a little boy was taking a walk with his father at night. Noticing that some of the homes displayed a shining silver star in the front window, the boy asked his father what those silver stars meant and was told, "Parents place them in their windows to show they gave a son who died in the war." The father and son continued their walk out of the neighborhood into the country. The little boy, looking up into the dark sky and seeing just one bright star, asked, "Daddy, did *God* give a Son, too?"

Yes, he did. The heavenly Father allowed his only Son, Jesus, to die on a cross for our sins. The death of Christ gave God the victory in his war against Satan. And there is no greater demonstration of sacrificial love than that. When the heavenly Father did not spare Jesus at Calvary but gave him up for us all, he proved beyond any doubt that he is for us.

Still, some believers fear their exposure to the attacks of Satan may cause them to become spiritually lost. Paul meets these fears head on in the remainder of the eighth chapter of Romans. He shows us three results of having God on our side.

## Since God Is for Us, We Need Not Fear Accusation

The apostle asks in verse 33: "Who will bring a charge against God's elect?" We can think of some answers to that question. Satan, for one, accuses us before our heavenly Father. But the remainder of this verse puts us at ease when it says: "God is the one who justifies." *The Good News Bible* translates this verse, "Who will accuse God's chosen people? God himself declares them not guilty!"

Imagine walking into a courtroom and seeing a defendant standing before the judge on a charge of theft. You approach the bench and say, "Your honor, the defendant is guilty. He stole my car. I saw him do it. He even admitted it to me." But the judge replies, "You're too late. I've already declared him not guilty. The United States Constitution protects him against double jeopardy, so I'm compelled to set him free."

In the spiritual realm you and I are that defendant. Satan is the accuser. The judge of mankind has pronounced us innocent because we've placed our faith in Jesus Christ, who paid sin's penalty for us. The devil has no case against us.

Picture this scene on the judgment day: A sinner saved by grace through faith in Christ is brought before God's throne. Satan smiles and says, "Look at his *filth!* His heart is deceitful. His mind is corrupt. His mouth is an open grave."

"I see no filth," God replies. "He has been washed in the blood of the Lamb."

"Then look at his *flaws!*" Satan continues. "He has fallen short of the glory of God. He is far from perfect. He often neglected prayer, the Bible, and church. He failed to show love and kindness to many people in need."

God looks at the man and answers, "I see no flaws. He is dressed in the righteousness of my Son, and he stands faultless before me."

"Then look at the *facts*!" Satan screams in desperation. "This person has disobeyed you tens of thousands of times. He has broken your laws in his thoughts, words, and actions. He has lied, cheated, stolen, lusted, and cursed. He was arrested for drunk driving and selling drugs. I can give you a whole book of dates and times to document these facts."

"The only fact I see," God says, "is that his name is written in the Book of Life. The catalog of his sins was erased when he trusted my Son, Jesus, as his personal Savior."

And thus even our archenemy who accuses us day and night has no foothold in the courtroom of God. We need not fear his accusations. Because God is for us, Satan is silenced.

### Since God Is for Us, We Need Not Fear Condemnation

In verse 34 Paul asks a new question: "Who is the one who condemns?" Again, we can think of possible answers. But none of them carries any weight when God is for us. The question, "Who is the one who condemns?" reminds us of the opening of this eighth chapter of Romans: "There is therefore now no condemnation for those who are in Christ Jesus." In this life we experience plenty of temptation and tribulation, but we will never suffer condemnation.

In the remainder of verse 34 Paul states four facts that back up his claim. First, "Christ Jesus is He who died." God cannot punish for the same offense twice. Because Jesus took our punishment for us when he died on the cross, we will not suffer the second death if our trust is in him.

Second, we cannot be condemned, because Christ "was raised." If the head is above water, the foot cannot drown. We believers are the body of Christ, of which he is the head. Because he rose to newness of life, we will, too. Death will lead us not into condemnation but into eternal salvation.

Third, we do not have to worry about being condemned, because our Lord "is at the right hand of God." This is the place of highest honor and greatest safety. And since we are in Christ as members of his body, we are also at God's right hand—the last place imaginable from which someone can be sent to hell.

Fourth, we will not be condemned, because Jesus "also intercedes for us." Sometimes we think of Christ as our judge. But Paul says he is our defense attorney. Can you conceive of the heavenly Father denying the pleas of the exalted Christ? I can't. And the exciting news is that he pleads for us. Charles Wesley wrote of this heavenly intercession:

> He ever lives above, for me to intercede,
> His all-redeeming love, His precious blood to plead.
> His blood atoned for all our race,
> And sprinkles now the throne of grace.
>
> Five bleeding wounds He bears, received on Calvary;
> They pour effectual prayers, they strongly plead for me.
> "Forgive him, O forgive," they cry,
> "Nor let that ransomed sinner die!"
>
> The Father hears Him pray, His dear anointed One,
> He cannot turn away the presence of His Son;
> His Spirit answers to the blood,
> And tells me I am born of God.
>
> —Charles Wesley, 1742

Having God on our side through faith in Christ assures us that we will not be condemned. But Paul suspects that some believers will invent still another excuse to fear. So he advances his thought once more.

## Since God Is for Us, We Need Not Fear Separation

In verse 35 the apostle asks, "Who shall separate us from the love of Christ?" He then lists seven possible answers. First is tribulation. Joseph experienced that when his brothers sold him into slavery and Potiphar's wife falsely accused him of attempted rape. He even spent two years in prison for a crime he did not commit. Joseph, did tribulation separate you from Christ's love? I hear him reply, "No! They meant these things for evil, but God meant them all for my good."

Second is distress. The Greek term for this is "a narrow place." Daniel was cooped up for a night in a cramped lions' den. Daniel, did the distress of that lions' den drive a wedge between you and God's love? And he answers, "The love of God closed the lions' mouths."

Third is persecution. Let's ask Stephen, the first Christian martyr, who was stoned to death for his faith, if Christ's love died out with him. "No!" he replies. "While the rocks crushed against my skull, I saw Jesus rise from his throne to welcome me into heaven."

Fourth is famine. Jacob, you almost perished during the seven years' famine recorded in Genesis. Did that make you doubt God's love? "At the time I thought everything was against me," he replies, "but in the end the famine served to reunite me with my son Joseph, who I thought was dead. God was for me, even when I nearly starved to death."

Fifth is nakedness. Job, when a tornado took the lives of

your ten children, you tore off your clothes and said, "Naked I came from my mother's womb, and naked I shall return there." Did you mean that you had been stripped of God's love? "No," he answers, "even then I knew that my Redeemer lived, and that in my body I would see God."

Sixth is peril or danger. David, you encountered years of that when you were dodging Saul's spears and hiding from him in caves. Several times you barely escaped with your life. Did that peril convince you that God no longer loved you? "No," he says, "my divine Shepherd prepared a table before me even in the presence of my enemies. Surely goodness and mercy followed me all the days of my life."

Finally, Paul mentions the sword. John the Baptist, Herod cut your head off with one of those. Were you suffering a punishment for your sins? His shout returns from heaven, "No, because by faith I had already beheld the Lamb of God, who takes away the sin of the world.

In verse 37 Paul joins the chorus of these biblical heroes when he says, "But in all these things we overwhelmingly conquer through Him who loved us." The King James Version says we are "more than conquerors." A conqueror defeats his enemy. To accomplish *more* than that is to turn your enemy into a friend. That's exactly what Jesus had done to Paul. He transformed his bitterest foe into his closest friend. The rebellious sinner became a redeemed saint. The persecutor of the church became a preacher of the gospel. The murderer of Christ's witnesses traveled to the ends of the earth as a missionary. Jesus was more than a conqueror in Paul's life.

And so are we in all our hardships. God uses trials to build our faith. In weakness we are made strong. In sickness we are able to minister to others as never before. Our losses become our gains. Even death ushers us into our Lord's eternal presence. Trials, far from separating us from Christ, drive us to him for help and strength. That makes us more than conquerors of all our troubles.

In verses 38 and 39 the apostle brings his argument to a climax: "For I am convinced that neither death, nor life, nor angels, nor principalities, nor things present, nor things to come, nor powers, nor height, nor depth, nor any other created thing, shall be able to separate us from the love of God, which is in Christ Jesus our Lord."

Paul sets the tone with his opening words, "I am convinced." Every Christian can and ought to enjoy this assurance that nothing can stand between him and Christ's love. He writes the potential dividers mostly in pairs. First is "death" and "life." Can you think of anything that is neither dead nor alive? Death is the first enemy that entered the world and the last one that will be destroyed, but even it cannot separate us from Christ's love.

Next, Paul speaks of "angels" and "principalities." That means good and evil spirits, angels and demons. No unseen powers of any kind will isolate us from Christ and his love.

Next are "things present" and "things to come." Nothing in this life or the next can sever us from the love of our Lord. Notice that Paul mentions the present and the future, but not the past. Many people allow the past with its sin, rebellion, and irreversible mistakes to interfere with their spiritual life. But Paul omits it here because the past life of the Christian no longer exists. Remember 2 Corinthians 5:17: "Therefore if any man is in Christ, he is a new creature; the old things passed away; behold, new things have come."

Then the apostle brings in "powers." Perhaps there is a pun here, as if Paul had said, "If you feel threatened by any other spiritual power, rest assured that it, too, is powerless when it comes to disconnecting you from God's love."

Next, are "height" and "depth." Nothing from heaven to hell can stand between us and the Savior.

Many thoughtful people have read these verses and said, "That's right; nothing can separate me from the love of Christ. But I can separate myself." Even that possibility is ruled out by the end of the list, which reads, "nor any other created thing." That includes you and me. Therefore, even we are incapable of removing ourselves from the warmth of Christ's love. We had no part in earning it, and we can have no part in losing it.

> Once in Christ, in Christ forever,
> Nothing from His love can sever.

## Personal Application

This great question, "If God is for us, who is against us?" is only part of Romans 8:31. The rest of the verse reads: "What then shall we say to these things?" I'd like to answer that question, too. We should say, "Father, since you are for me, I pledge to be for you."

First, we see that since God is for us we need not fear accusation. Not only will our Lord not accuse us of sin once we are forgiven in Christ, but even the devil's vicious indictments will fall to the ground.

Therefore, let's bring to a halt our own accusations against our heavenly Father. When temptations have been strong we have accused him of giving us more than we can handle, in spite of his promise in 1 Corinthians 10:13 to keep the tug of our temptations below our threshold of resistance. When a family member has died we have charged the Lord with injustice and even cruelty. When he has denied our prayer requests for our own good we have accused him of failing to listen to us and failing to care about our happiness. All this is evidence that we have not been on God's side. If we are for Christ we must put away all our accusations against him, just as he swept away all of his and even the devil's against us.

Second, this text teaches us that because God is for us, we need not fear condemnation. The opposite of condemnation is salvation. Therefore, to be totally for God means we will spread the message of Christ's salvation to people who are lost in sin. Condemnation is not merely a doctrine in God's Word; it is a reality in our world. People you know and love are on their way to hell, because they have not trusted Jesus as their personal Savior. The greatest thing we can do for Christ is to share his gospel of free and full salvation unashamedly with people who desperately need to hear it. Will you do that?

Finally, since God is for us, we need not fear separation. Therefore, to prove that we are for God we must cling to Christ, no matter what the consequences may be. We must promise, "Jesus, I am yours. Nothing will ever separate you from my love."

God is for you. Are you for him? Or do you prove by your murmuring, your lack of witnessing, and your distance from Christ that you are against him? When you understand that God is for you, all unholy fear is swept away. And when you know that you are for God, you enjoy the purpose for which you were created.

# 10

## A Question of Requirements

"What does the LORD your God require from you?" (Deut. 10:12)

When students enter a new class they usually ask, "What are the requirements? How many tests will there be? Will we have to write a term paper? And if so, how long must it be?" These were typical questions in my classes from grade school through graduate school.

It's the same in the workplace. Employees need to know when their employers want them to start work in the morning, how much output is expected of them, and even how quickly they must return from lunch and coffee breaks. Everybody wants to know the requirements.

Including Christians. And God is happy to satisfy our

curiosity. In Deuteronomy 10:12 Moses asks, "And now, Israel, what does the LORD your God require from you?" No doubt we can take "the LORD your God" in this verse to mean "Jesus Christ." Christians should always read the Old Testament with New Testament eyes, and the New Testament clearly teaches that Jesus is both Lord (Rom. 10:9) and God (Matt. 1:23; Heb. 1:8). So Deuteronomy 10:12 expresses our responsibility to Christ.

Also, we should keep in mind that this text addresses people who already know God. It therefore speaks of requirements for *living* the Christian life, not *entering* it. If Jesus is not yet your Savior, you are not ready for Deuteronomy 10:12. A better verse for you would be 1 John 3:23: "This is His commandment, that we believe in the name of His Son Jesus Christ."

Following are God's five requirements of Christians.

### Fear Him

Deuteronomy 10:12 begins, "And now, Israel, what does the LORD your God require from you, but to fear the LORD your God?" Many Bible teachers are quick to say that *fear* means "respect" or "reverence." They point out that Christians should not be afraid of God, because he is their heavenly Father. Whereas a slave may fear his master, a child should not feel the same way about his or her loving father.

But this is an oversimplification. Of course we should respect and reverence our Lord. But fear can also be healthy. Sometimes it is the only thing that motivates people to fulfill their obligations. Children quickly pick up their scattered toys when dad threatens to discipline them. A student burns the midnight oil when he is on the verge of failing a class. A star athlete may take practice for granted until another player challenges his position in the starting lineup. An employee may be lazy until he hears rumors of a layoff.

I think the contemporary church has lost the fear of the Lord. The average Christian today has a casual attitude toward God and his Son, Jesus. He doesn't dread the consequences of neglecting Scripture, prayer, or the Lord's Day. Many believers can even sin in more notorious ways and think nothing of it.

I know a Christian who tried to justify himself by saying, "Even though I am sinning, I'm not going to lose my salvation over it. The worst that can happen is that I'll lose my fellowship with the Lord." But is that an insignificant thing? A disciple in a healthy state of heart would dread the thought of forfeiting his intimacy with Christ. When many of us should be trembling we are trifling.

Do you shudder at the thought of offending a holy God? If not, then you have failed the Lord's first requirement.

## Walk in All His Ways

Verse 12 goes on to say that God requires us to "walk in all His ways." To walk with someone is to be close to him or her. How is your fellowship with the Lord? When my wife and I go for walks, we find that it helps us to communicate. In the home we have the distractions of the children, the telephone, and the television. But a walk frees us to nurture our relationship.

Walking implies several things. One is *action*. Walking is the opposite of sitting and doing nothing. Are you a Christian? Then act like it. Live the things you believe. Let others see your faith at work. Get moving in your spiritual life.

Second, walking implies *progress*. If you take one step and then sit down, that's not much of a walk. Are you growing in Christ? Are you more spiritually mature than you were a year ago? If not, why not? Every disciple should be on the grow.

Third, walking implies *perseverance*. Scripture says that "Enoch walked with God three hundred years" until the Lord "took him" (Gen. 5:22, 24). We can be sure that many obstacles to his faith confronted Enoch during those three centuries. But he did not give up. He continued walking with God. Often I meet people who say, "I used to live for Christ, but then such and such happened." Maybe they yielded to a severe temptation, or they grew complacent toward Christ over the years, or their pastor left his wife for another woman and became a stumbling block to them. But God expects us to persevere through every obstacle as we walk with him.

Finally, walking implies *habit*. We cannot claim to walk in the Lord's ways if we merely show up at church on Sunday and then for all practical purposes forget him the rest of the week. If we are going to walk with Christ we must cling to him every day. We must be in a constant spirit of prayer. And the Bible must be our daily guide in decision making.

In Paul's letter to the Ephesians the word *walk* has two different applications. In chapter 2, verse 2 he says, "You formerly walked according to . . . the prince of the power of the air." That, of course, is Satan. In Ephesians 5:8 he writes, "Now you are light in the Lord; walk as children of light." Do you see the contrast? If we do not walk with Christ we walk with the devil. There is no middle ground. Who is your spiritual companion? With whom do you walk?

### Love Him

Deuteronomy 10:12 goes on to say that our Lord requires us to "love Him," the third of five requirements God lays out in this passage and the central one. Jesus said the greatest commandment of all is that we love God with everything we have (Matt. 22:37–38). It stands to reason, then, that not loving him must be the greatest sin.

The previous requirement is that we walk in all God's ways. Walking with Christ without love in our hearts makes fellowship a chore. This is why many people who go to church, read their Bibles every day, and say their prayers find it boring. They walk in God's ways, all right, but without love in their hearts. However, when we sincerely love Christ, the walk becomes sweet.

If we love Christ we are not content to wander from him or rebel against him. Love for our Lord enables us to trust him. If we love him we suffer cheerfully for him. We love the things that are dear to him, such as his Word, his people, and his day.

We can be sure of this: If Jesus is not the object of our affections, something or someone else is. But is it worthy of our love? Certainly not as worthy as Christ. He gave us the ability to love in the first place, so we should love him above everything and everyone else.

A fifteenth-century Christian compared God's demand for our love to wings on a bird. The wings seem to add weight to the body, but in reality they lift it into the air. When the Lord comes along and commands us to love him, our human nature sees that as a burden. But on the contrary, love lifts our spirits up to heavenly things. If you take away a bird's wings, it cannot fly. And if we refuse to love Christ we become incapable of living differently from non-Christians.

## Serve Him

The fourth of God's requirements is found at the end of verse 12: "Serve the LORD your God with all your heart and

with all your soul." Note the connection: Because we love
Jesus we must serve him. It would be wrong for our love to
do nothing. True affection always longs to show itself in
action.

This text demands wholehearted service to the Lord. It
calls us to serve "with all your heart and with all your
soul." If we take the word *serve* out of *service,* all that's left
is *ice.* And a lot of Christians need defrosting.

Many Christians have a narrow view of ministry. They
pronounce *service* as "serve *us.*" They suppose that the pastor is the one who serves God. Their job, they think, is to
be spectators. Not so! Ephesians 4:12 clearly teaches that
the work of ministry belongs to every believer.

Lloyd Ogilvie, pastor of Hollywood Presbyterian Church,
once said in an interview, "We do not allow the people of
our congregation to call us on the staff 'the ministers.' We
want everyone in the church to consider himself or herself
a minister of God." Anthony Evans, pastor of Oak Cliffe
Bible Fellowship in Dallas, says that when people go
through his newcomers class, he only accepts them into the
membership if they sign up for a ministry.

What's your ministry, your area of service to Christ? Do
you have a responsibility in your church, and are you faithful to it? When was the last time you brought someone to
church with you? Do you speak of Christ to others, both
verbally and with your life? I think sharing the gospel of
our Lord with people who need to hear it is the highest service we can render.

Jesus sweat blood for us. Can't we sweat a little bit for
him? His hands and feet were pierced for us. Will our hands
do nothing for him? Will our feet stay put? In the sixteenth
century Ignatius uttered a prayer that we do well to repeat:
"Teach us, Lord, to serve You as You deserve: to give and not

to count the cost, to fight and not to heed the sounds, to labor and not to look for rest, to work and not to ask for any reward, except that of knowing we are doing Your will."

## Obey Him

The fifth and final requirement of God is given in Deuteronomy 10:12 and 13: "What does the LORD your God require from you, but . . . to keep the LORD's commandments and His statutes which I am commanding you today for your good?" Scripture is full of accounts of people who tried to offer God partial obedience. But he always treated it as disobedience.

The Lord told Saul, the first King of Israel, to destroy the Amalekites. They were ripe for judgment, and God wanted Israel to be his sword of vengeance. But Saul only partially obeyed. As a result, the Lord said, "I regret that I have made Saul king, for he has turned back from following Me, and has not carried out My commands" (1 Sam. 15:1–11). Saul's partial obedience dethroned him.

It was second down, and the ball was resting on their own three-yard line. The coach's plan was to get his team away from the goal line so they'd have room to punt. During a time-out he told his quarterback, "Hand off to Jones, our big fullback, for the next two plays. Then punt." The young quarterback did as he was instructed. On the first play he gave the ball to Jones, who found a hole off tackle and ran fifty yards. The same play was called again, and to the coach's surprise the hole opened up like before. This time Jones ran forty-five yards. The fans were delirious. The ball was on the opponents' two-yard line, just six feet from the goal.

The coach could hardly believe his eyes when he saw the

quarterback punt the ball into the bleachers on the next play. As the quarterback came off the field, the coach angrily grabbed him and screamed, "What in the world were you thinking when you called that last play?" The young man answered bluntly, "I was thinking what a dumb coach we have."

At least we have to give that quarterback credit for obeying authority, even when he thought he had a better idea. He didn't question his leader, even if he couldn't understand his orders. That's what God is looking for in us his children.

In his book *Of God and Men,* A. W. Tozer writes, "There is scarcely anything so dull and meaningless as Bible doctrine taught for its own sake. No man is better for knowing that God in the beginning created heaven and earth. The devil knows that, and so did Ahab and Judas Iscariot. No man is better for knowing that God so loved the world that He gave His only begotten Son to die for their redemption. In hell there are millions who know that. Theological truth is useless until it is obeyed" (pp. 26, 27).

Ironically, Satan's children put most of God's children to shame when it comes to obedience. They follow the devil in total commitment, while we play fast and loose with the heavenly Father. This is why our enemy seems to have the advantage in this world. We Christians are often in disarray, while Satan's troops are lined up ready for action. And tragically, most of them don't even realize that they are pawns in the devil's hands.

Obedience is like love; we give it to somebody. God made us that way. But we only find fulfillment in life if we submit to the right master. That's what Moses means at the end of Deuteronomy 10:13 where he says that God gives commandments "for your good." A look at Deuteronomy 5:29

and 6:24 shows this is the third time Moses has stressed the point.

Sometimes we assume that the divine law is a heavy burden. But Jesus said, "My yoke is easy, and My load is light" (Matt. 11:30). We think we know what's best for us. But if we submit to Christ's law we will be better off.

Some teenagers presume that happiness is found in drugs. But then those drugs cause death at an early age. If they only listen to their parents they can enjoy life. The counsel they despise is for their own good. And so it is with us, God's children. The commands he gives us to obey are for our own good. If we choose to do our own thing we only hurt and destroy ourselves.

## Personal Application

I think these five requirements can be reduced to one: *God requires total commitment from us.* But that still leaves us with a nagging question: Just *how* do we fulfill these requirements? By setting our jaws, clenching our fists, and giving it our best effort? No, that only leads to failure. However good our intentions may be, we always fall short in our own strength. The only way to carry out our heavenly Father's demands is to allow Christ to do it through us. If you are a Christian, Jesus already lives *in* you. But does he live *through* you? Is his life your source of power? Are you surrendered to his control? In the end, the Lord only asks us to do that for which he himself supplies the power.

One last thought. The word *requirements* implies that we pay a penalty if we don't fulfill them. What is that penalty? I believe it is divine discipline. Whenever we fail to live in holy fear, stray in our walk with Christ, grow indifferent, idle, and disobedient, God doesn't let us get away with it for long. He has his ways of getting us back into line. In the end it's easier to be committed to Christ than to face the responsibilities of not being committed.

Does that inspire some fear in you? Good! Because that puts you back at the starting point of God's requirements. And once you take that first step, you are on the road to fulfilling the other four.

# 11

# A Question of Robbery

"Will a man rob God?" (Mal. 3:8)

One Sunday morning in the Walnut Creek Church of Reno, Nevada, several masked men with guns interrupted the service. They shouted, "Everybody do what we say, and no one will get hurt! If you attempt any heroics, we'll shoot to kill!" Pastor Roy Sykes calmly told the worshipers to cooperate. In ten minutes the thieves had made their getaway with all the money and jewelry of the congregants.

Sounds outrageous, doesn't it? Have you ever been present in a church service when robbers entered the sanctuary? No doubt you have. Perhaps you have even been the thief. Now, before you take offense at my accusation, listen to what our Lord says in Malachi 3:8: "Will a man rob

God? Yet you are robbing Me! But you say, 'How have we robbed Thee?' In tithes and offerings."

## The Crime

The crime in this verse is stealing from God by failing to give him a tithe of one's income. *Tithe* is an Old English word that means a "tenth." Ten percent of our income is the smallest amount ever commanded in the Bible for giving to the Lord. We may think that people who donate a tenth of their salary to God are extraordinary Christians. But all they really prove is that they are not thieves.

In 1985 the average yearly income for a welfare recipient was $7,500. Ten percent of that is $750. During that same year in a major evangelical denomination the average adult gave $440. So even if everyone had been on welfare, the total giving would have averaged out to less than a tithe. Imagine what percentage of their actual income they gave! What can this mean but the average church is made up of many members who are guilty of theft?

One afternoon years ago, while working in my office, I heard police sirens. They screamed louder and louder, until the patrol cars pulled into our church parking lot. Soon the police were opening the door to our sanctuary! There some teenagers were caught stealing expensive sound equipment. The officers had been tipped off by one of the kids' acquaintances.

I was doubly dumbfounded; first, because anyone would steal from a church, and second, because the culprits were part of our congregation. I thought to myself, "How can these young people rob a church that has nurtured them since childhood?" I was beginning to feel something of Malachi's astonishment when he wrote, "Will a man rob God?"

In a later experience, one of our Sunday school teachers caught two girls taking money from her purse. I told them how disappointed and surprised I was that they would steal from the woman who had taught them God's Word. But how much more shocking it is that we should rob God himself!

Some time ago I talked with a pastor who confessed to me that he pilfered money from his church's funds. Though I tried not to show it, I was aghast. But Malachi tells me that case wasn't so rare after all. I detect a gasp of shock in his question: "Will a man rob God?" It was as if he were saying, "Is this the way redeemed people treat the Lord who purchased their salvation?"

I have another friend in the ministry who bought a new house and then almost sold it because he was having difficulty paying his tithes and offerings. He told me that if his monthly mortgage ever prevented him from giving his tithe to God, he would sell the house and rent an inexpensive apartment, even though he would lose equity in the future. That's the kind of commitment that honors the Lord and that the Lord honors in return.

Christian, if you are guilty of stealing from God, repent of it. Yes, repentance is for believers, too. Don't take your neglect of the tithe lightly. It's nothing less than grand larceny against the judge of the universe.

## The Command

In the tenth verse our Lord tells us how to cease being thieves: "Bring the whole tithe into the storehouse." Some believers say this command has nothing to do with us in the age of grace. They argue that tithing is an Old Testament law that has been set aside by Jesus Christ.

But we may only label an Old Testament practice outdated if the New Testament gives us a license to do so. For example, we do not adhere to the many food laws that Moses gave, because the Gospels tell us that Jesus "declared all foods clean" (Mark 7:19). Nor do we sacrifice lambs, because Christ is "the Lamb of God who takes away the sin of the world" (John 1:29). Priests were the mediators between God and men in the Old Testament. But according to 1 Timothy 2:5 Jesus is now our only mediator. These practices are explicitly superseded in the New Testament. Yet nowhere do we read that tithing has been set aside.

But some Christians are quick to point out that the apostle Paul never used the words *tithe* or *tithing*. That is true, though he did speak of generous and sacrificial giving, particularly by those in poverty (2 Cor. 8:1–4), which sounds like more than tithing. I'm inclined to believe that Paul did not mention the giving of 10 percent, because Christians were going far beyond that. Believers were selling their houses and dedicating the profits to the Lord's work (Acts 4:34–35).

Even if tithing were merely an Old Testament law, shouldn't we New Testament believers freely give at least 10 percent to our Lord? We enjoy so many more advantages than the Jews who lived before Christ. We owe him a greater debt of love. Why then do we complain when the subject of tithing comes up?

Some people teach new Christians to start with a small percentage and work up to a tithe. The first year you may give 3 percent, the next year 4 percent, and so on until you reach the level of 10 percent. But Malachi tells us that God wants the *whole* tithe, and he wants it *now*. The prophet's contemporaries were not hoarding all their money. They were giving to the Lord. But it wasn't the whole tithe. And because they withheld part of it, they were guilty of stealing.

Imagine telling a new Christian who had a promiscuous background, "God will be pleased with you if you cut back on your adultery to just once a week. Work your way up to freedom from your marital unfaithfulness over the course of five years." Imagine allowing a compulsive liar who had just trusted Christ a quota of fewer and fewer lies each month until he finally learned to tell the truth. Imagine instructing a thief to taper off on his bank robbing now that he's a Christian. No, we tell new converts to repent of their former sins *now*. And in the same way, even a new believer can and should render to his Lord at least 10 percent of his income. Percentage giving below the tithe is theft. And to everyone who practices it, Ephesians 4:28 says, "Let him who steals steal no longer."

Our text also strikes a death blow to the excuse that some people are too poor to yield 10 percent of their income to the Lord. In Malachi 3:11 devouring locusts were destroying the crops of the Jews, and the grapes were shriveling before they became ripe. If anyone had a right to complain of an inability to tithe, it was Malachi's contemporaries. But God made no exception in their case.

A woman who worshiped in a church I used to serve was married to a man who was sent to prison for several felony counts. The wife had to sell their house and virtually all her belongings to pay her husband's legal fees. Then she and her two children went on welfare. Her friends urged her to give up her habit of tithing. They said God would understand that she couldn't give 10 percent now. Uncertain of what she should do, she came to me for advice.

With much fear and trembling, I told her I found in the Bible no exceptions to the rule of tithing. I reminded her of the widow who was preparing a last meal for her son and herself before they were to die of starvation. Elijah came along and asked her to give him that final meal. She did, and from that point on God provided miraculously for her and her son. I told my friend that she served the same heavenly Father, who was just as worthy of her trust. Encouraged, she left my office that day determined to rely on her Lord to provide for her and her two children as she continued tithing. And he did provide. That mother's faith was continually tested, but God proved himself worthy of her trust.

The only poverty that prevents us from tithing is a poverty of faith in God to supply our needs while we obey his commands. Sell your television set if you have to but don't rob God. Eat less if you have to. Give up your membership at the exercise club if you have to. Mow your own lawn and wash your own car instead of paying other people to do those things if you have to. But don't rob God.

The Associated Press ran an article about Pastor Conrad Willard of the Central Baptist Church of Miami, Florida. He offered refunds of up to $2,000 to anyone who started tithing and became dissatisfied. In the more than ten years since he made the offer, none of the 4,000 members of his church requested refunds. Instead, the number of people who pledged to tithe increased dramatically.

God can stretch ninety cents farther than we can stretch a dollar. But can we trust him for that?

In this tenth verse the Lord demands that we present the *whole* tithe to him. Let's remember that obedience to God must always go beyond the letter to the spirit of the command. It's not enough to write out the check for 10 percent of our incomes. We must also give it cheerfully. Otherwise, we have not given the whole tithe. Second Corinthians 9:7 reminds us that "God loves a cheerful giver."

I can see it now. As the offering prayer is spoken in church, a man begrudgingly pulls a check out of his pocket. Then he seems to hear God say, "Is that all you're giving me?"

"But Lord," he answers, "this is a tithe!"

"I want the whole tithe," God replies, "and that includes more than just money. I want you to give me the right attitude as well as the right amount. Your tithe is incomplete, because I find no cheerfulness in it."

You can be nagged about tithing. But until the Holy Spirit changes your heart, there will always be something missing. Cheerfulness is an indispensable part of your stewardship. So ask God to put gladness into your giving; that's what he loves to see.

## The Consequence

What is the result of obeying this command? Malachi 3:10 supplies the answer: "'Test Me now in this,' says the LORD of hosts, 'if I will not open for you the windows of heaven, and pour out for you a blessing until it overflows.'"

God's overflowing blessing is the consequence of our faithful giving. Mark how he invites us to put him to the test in this regard. Often people have wished they could prove the existence of God in a test tube. Now our heavenly Father extends to us that kind of opportunity. He says, "If you doubt my ability to supply your needs, put me to the test. If you fear that I will make your life miserable, experiment with me and see what kind of God I really am. Please try me out. Give me a chance to prove myself to you."

Ironically, by demanding that we test him, God tests us. The windows of heaven swing on the hinges of our obedience. The fullness of our Lord's blessing depends on the fullness of our tithes.

Notice how the heavenly Father urges us to test him "now." There's no better time to change your ways than right now. If God is softening your heart today, don't wait until tomorrow to respond to him. Tomorrow your heart may be harder.

The apostle Paul made a similar promise on the Lord's behalf when he wrote: "And my God shall supply all your needs according to his riches in glory in Christ Jesus" (Phil.4:19). Often we seize the promises of Scripture without remembering their conditions. The Philippian church had sacrificed several times to support Paul in his missionary endeavors. That's why they could count on God to supply their every need. The promises of God's overflowing blessing in Malachi and his all sufficient supply in Philippians do not apply to every Christian. They can only be claimed by faithful, obedient disciples.

We should not limit the overflowing blessing of Malachi 3:10 to mean financial sufficiency. God has much more in store for us than that. We also receive the blessings of pleasing our Lord, knowing we're doing his will, having his joy in our hearts, and helping to advance his gospel in our needy world.

I think the most fulfilling blessing that comes from generous giving is that it conforms us more to the image of our Lord Jesus. Often we pray to be Christ-like in our love. But how did Jesus prove his love for us? By giving himself. John 15:13 says it all: "Greater love has no one than this, that one lay down his life for his friends." And that's precisely what Christ did for us. He proved his love by giving up his life for us on Calvary's cross.

The purest form of giving is the giving of yourself. When you do that, anything else you give—whether it be time, money, friendship, or sympathy—will be bathed in love. Then you will have measurable evidence that God is conforming you to the image of his Son. That's the highest blessing of giving.

## Personal Application

How would you feel if your neighbor told you that your son or daughter had stolen something from him? You would be grieved. That's how I feel when God accuses his people of stealing from him. So don't blame me for this message. I didn't write the Malachi text. I'm only attempting to restore your fellowship with Christ by helping you overcome the sin of robbing God.

This is not a financial issue at all; it's a spiritual one. I challenge the claim of anyone who says his spiritual life is in order when he has not surrendered his finances to the Lord. Tithing is not a fund-raising scheme. Its purpose is not to give the church a way to secure possessions, but to give God a way to secure people. It's not our wealth he's after but us.

In his book *Your Money Matters,* Malcolm MacGregor writes: "One of two things is going to happen with the tithe—it will either be given to God or it will be collected by Satan. People ask, 'What do you mean, "It will be collected by Satan"?' I mean it will go for things that have absolutely no lasting value" Malcolm MacGregor, *Your Money Matters* (Minneapolis: Bethany Fellowship, 1977), p. 47.

That challenges me. I don't want to surrender any part of my life to the devil. I long to make a difference that will count for all eternity. How about you?

# 12

## A Question of Ownership

"Or do you not know that your body is a temple of the Holy Spirit who is in you, whom you have from God, and that you are not your own?" (1 Cor. 6:19)

If you are a person of average size, every twenty-four hours your heart beats 103,680 times. You breathe 23,040 times. You inhale 438 cubic feet of air. You eat about three and one-half pounds of food, and drink almost three pints of liquid. No matter what the weather conditions, your body maintains a temperature close to 98.6 degrees (F). You generate 450 tons of energy. You use seven million brain cells. In the course of your daily routine, you walk about five miles. If you are a man, you speak 12,000 words; if a woman, 23,000 words.

But what is the body ultimately for? Eating and drinking? Pampering with a cushy lifestyle? Is it to be used as a tempting bait to lure the opposite sex? No. First Corinthians 6:19–20 teaches that our physical bodies belong to God, and therefore we are to use them to glorify him.

## Our Relationship with God

First Corinthians 6:19 points out two truths about our relationship with God.

### He Occupies Our Bodies

The apostle Paul asks the Corinthian believers, "Or do you not know that your body is a temple of the Holy Spirit who is in you, whom you have from God?" This is the sixth time in 1 Corinthians 6 that Paul has asked his readers a question with the words *Do you not know.* He is astonished that some of his fellow Christians do not realize their bodies are the temples of God's Spirit.

Today, also, many Christians have not grasped this truth. But that does not change the fact that whether you realize it or not, the Holy Spirit moves into your heart and sets up his temple in your body when you trust Jesus as your personal Savior.

Many new believers who haven't yet heard of the Holy Spirit invite him into their hearts later on when they learn of him. To them he is a second blessing after conversion. Then they ask other Christians, "Have you been baptized with the Holy Spirit?" Their question assumes that a believer in Christ does not possess God's Spirit if he did not pray to be indwelt by the Spirit when he was converted. But Scripture teaches that the Holy Spirit occupies the body of every Christian. Romans 8:9 clearly states that "if anyone does not have the Spirit of Christ, he does not belong to Him (Christ)."

The Old Testament temple was the earthly dwelling place of God. Since the Holy Spirit lives in a temple, we can conclude that he is divine. We can also say that in the Old Testament God had a temple for his people, whereas in the New Testament God has his people for a temple. Think of it; if you are a Christian your physical body is the Holy of Holies, the temple of God himself.

The failure of many Christians to grasp this awesome reality is illustrated by the story of a boy who was sitting in the front row of his church, intently listening to his pastor preach. He was also chewing bubblegum quite loudly, much to the disgust of an elderly woman in a nearby pew.

After the service she complained to the pastor, "I was shocked at the smacking of that boy's lips. Did you notice that he was chewing gum in the house of God?"

"Madam," the pastor replied, "the house of God was chewing gum."

Yes, we are God's house, his temple. Do you live as though it is true? The Old Testament temple was wholly dedicated to God's use. Whether you live and work in a factory, an office, a school, a farm, or a department store, the heavenly Father wants you to be totally committed to serving Christ there in a holy way.

Immediately before this verse Paul cautioned the Corinthians against sex outside marriage. One of the outrageous features of ancient pagan religions was the use of temple prostitutes. Men would pay to enter a heathen shrine and have sex with a harlot as an act of worship. Talk about temple desecration! Yet that's the kind of perversion Christians entangle themselves in when they fall into sexual sin. God never designed his temple for that kind of use. He expects us to be clean, holy habitations from which the splendor of his glory can shine in all its brilliance.

We must also pause to take stock of the contaminants we put into this flesh-and-blood temple. Last year Americans spent more than $20 billion on cigarettes. Former Surgeon General C. Everett Koop reported that smoking causes more than one in every six deaths in the United States. Dr. Gerald Fletcher, director of internal medicine at Georgia Baptist Hospital in Atlanta, testifies that "every cigarette smoked by a person takes eleven minutes off his life." And former Health, Education, and Welfare Secretary Joseph Califano described smoking as "slow-motion suicide." Obviously, it defiles and destroys God's human temple.

Soon after I bought my first home, I built a fire in the fireplace. But I forgot to open the flue, and smoke started backing up into the house. I immediately corrected my mistake, and although the smoke rose into my living room for only a few seconds, I was afraid it might stain my clean walls. It occurred to me that the Holy Spirit must also desire to live in an unpolluted house. Yet many believers dump all kinds of filth down the chimney of his temple.

Including alcohol. The United States uses enough grain—5.2 million tons—in the production of alcoholic beverages every year to feed 26 million starving people. (reported by Ronald J. Sider in *The Graduated Tithe,* [Downers Grove, Ill.: InterVarsity Press], 24).

If the Old Testament Jews scrupulously prevented unclean things from entering their temple, how much more should we New Testament believers do the same. Because God occupies our bodies, we should preserve them in holiness.

### He Owns Our Bodies

Paul's question continues at the end of 1 Corinthians 6:19: "Or do you not know . . . that you are not your own?" Some of the believers in Corinth did not know that. They failed to realize they had no right to do whatever they wanted with their bodies. And today many people are still ignorant of this fact. One of the major arguments for abortion is that "a woman has a right to do what she wants with her own body." But it's *not* her own body; it belongs to God.

How would you feel if someone took a sledgehammer to your car and smashed it? You'd have every right to be angry, because it's your car, not his. In the same way, every body belongs to God. We are not our own. So we have no right to damage the Lord's property by drunkenness, smoking, gluttony, drugs, or any other "sledgehammer."

"You are not your own." This applies to every area of life. Your *money* is not your own. God supplies your income and has the right to tell you what to do with it. Your *abilities* are not your own. The Holy Spirit has gifted you in a specific way and expects you to use your talents in service to Christ. Your *time* is not your own. Death proves that. So give your time generously to the Lord now in acknowledgment of his control over you. Your *possessions* are not your own. The heavenly Father holds title to your house, business, cars, clothes, television sets, and swimming pool. Your *heart* is not your own. That's why Scripture forbids you to give it to a non-Christian in marriage (1 Cor. 7:39; 2 Cor. 6:14). God wants you to yield your heart in love to another believer who is devoted to Christ.

This principle holds for unbelievers as well. Sometimes I hear Bible teachers say that non-Christians are free to reject Christ if they want to. Not so! It is no more anyone's privilege to reject the Savior than it is a student's privilege to cut class or a soldier's privilege to be absent without leave. If we had a right to refuse Christ, how could God punish us for doing it? His condemnation of people to eternal hell for saying no to his Son proves that they possess no such right.

A young woman once told Martin Luther she had sold her body to the devil.

"No you haven't," responded Luther, "for you are not your own. It's not your body to sell."

If you have no Savior in your heart, invite Jesus in now. You are obligated to do this, for you are not your own. And if you refuse, you must suffer the consequences.

## Our Redemption by God

The opening of verse 20 explains why we are not our own: "For you have been bought with a price." And what is that price? There can be only one answer: Christ's blood, shed on Calvary's cross, was the ransom price that delivered us from sin's grip. We read in 1 Peter 1:18–19: "You were not redeemed with perishable things like silver or gold from your futile way of life inherited from your forefathers, but with precious blood, as of a lamb unblemished and spotless, the blood of Christ." And in Revelation 5:9 we learn that the song of heaven is, "Thou wast slain, and didst purchase for God with Thy blood men from every tribe and tongue and people and nation."

Jesus' blood is the highest price ever paid in any transaction. Paul might have said, "You are not your own, for God created you." That would have made sense. But our salvation is a greater feat than our creation. The Lord created us with his word, but he redeemed us with his blood.

At age seventeen I experienced a brush with death. I had lost twenty-five pounds in one week and was about to slip into a coma. Then my doctor admitted me to the hospital where my sickness was successfully treated in minutes. I had become diabetic, but when they injected me with insulin, my body started functioning normally again. Ever since I've felt as if I've been living on borrowed time. Each day, when I inject my insulin, I'm reminded that God has given me another chance.

Christ's redemption of us is like that. We were perishing with the terminal disease of sin. Then Jesus came into our lives and administered his blood to our souls. All at once we were made whole. Let's never forget that we are former hostages whose freedom has been purchased. The ransom price has been paid in full with Christ's blood. Our Savior does not make payments over the course of years on a mortgage that Satan holds on us. He paid the entire price one day on a hill called Calvary. Now we are not our own. We rightfully belong to Jesus. Consequently, our hearts are filled with gratitude to God and we are able to sing along with James Gray in his hymn:

> Neither silver nor gold hath obtained my redemption,
> Nor riches of earth could have saved my poor soul.
> The blood of the cross is my only foundation,
> The death of my Savior now maketh me whole.
> I am redeemed, but not with silver;
> I am bought, but not with gold;
> Bought with a price—the blood of Jesus,
> Precious price of love untold.

## Our Responsibility to God

As a result of what Paul has said up to this point, he concludes in 1 Corinthians 6:20: "Therefore glorify God in your body." This command reveals that, although we are not our own, we possess great liberty. Before we placed our faith in Christ, we were slaves of sin. But now for the first

time we are free not to sin. And more than that, we are free
to serve our Lord rather than Satan.

How can we glorify God in our bodies? Let me make
some suggestions. The foremost way mentioned in the context of this command is by avoiding sexual sin. The city of
Corinth was famous for its disgraceful behavior in this area.
In the Greek language "to Corinthianize" meant "to commit sexual sin." And as you know, fornication, adultery, and
homosexuality are still rampant today.

Are you faithful to your husband or wife? When you are,
you not only make your spouse happy and keep yourself
clean, you glorify God. If you are single, are you saving
yourself for your future marriage partner? A best-selling
book for single people asks the question *Why Wait?* I'll give
you the best reason of all: It glorifies God. Maybe you
think, "What if I never marry anyone? Then there's no
spouse to save myself for." Okay, but you can save yourself
for Christ, and that will glorify him in your body.

You can also glorify God in your body by means of reg-
ular exercise, sufficient sleep, and moderate eating habits.
You can bring glory to your Lord in a physical way by
refusing to indulge your human temple in smoking, drinking, and other habit-forming drugs. You can take your body
to church, bend it in prayer, and use your eyes to read his
Word and your mouth to witness to people who don't
know Christ. You need not be a pastor to glorify God with
your body, for Paul adds in 1 Corinthians 10:31: "Whether,
then, you eat or drink or whatever you do, do all to the
glory of God."

Notice how all three members of the Trinity appear at
the end of 1 Corinthians 6. God the Holy Spirit dwells in
us, as we saw in the first part of verse 19. At the beginning
of verse 20 is a reference to Jesus in the words *bought with*

*a price,* for it was his blood that purchased our salvation. Finally, we learned that our duty is to glorify God the Father. Thus, our obedience to this command affects the reputation of each person in the Godhead.

## Personal Application

In the first half of the nineteenth century a man visited the cathedral of Fribourg in Switzerland and asked to examine the organ. At first the attendant refused him permission, but after a great deal of persuasion he let him in. As the man began to play, the attendant stood spellbound. "Who are you?" he asked.

"My name is Felix Mendelssohn."

"Mendelssohn!" cried the attendant, lifting up his hands in amazement. "And to think that I refused to let you play the organ!"

Perhaps, like that attendant, you did not realize that the Holy Spirit has already set up his temple in your body. Maybe you didn't understand that he wants to compose a symphony out of your life that will glorify the heavenly Father throughout eternity. But now you do understand this. So I remind you of Paul's plea from Romans 12:1: "I urge you therefore, brethren, by the mercies of God, to present your bodies a living and holy sacrifice, acceptable to God, which is your spiritual service of worship."

But what if you have never given your life to Christ? Then your body is not God's temple, for the Holy Spirit does not dwell within you. Instead, sin is the only thing living in your heart. But it does not have to remain that way; you, too, have been bought with a price. And just like the Christian, "You are not your own."

Even nonbelievers are obligated to surrender themselves

to the Lord Jesus. So say the following prayer, first uttered by an old hymn writer:

> Not my own, my life, my body,
> Freely all to Christ I bring,
> To be used in joyful service
> For the glory of my King.
>
> —Author unknown

It makes perfect sense when you remember that every *body* belongs to God.

# 13

## A Question of Friendship

"Do you not know that friendship with the
world is hostility toward God?" (James 4:4).

Everyone needs friends, and I believe
everyone has them. The only friend some people know is a
dog or a cat. We say, "A dog is a man's best friend" and "A
diamond is a girl's best friend." A little girl who is shunned
by her schoolmates knows she will always be accepted by
her dolls. An ivory-tower scholar may find warm compan-
ionship in books. In one way or another, we all need and
enjoy friends.

An old saying has it that "any friend of yours is a friend
of mine." But what if my friend is your enemy? Does that
make me your enemy? If you were God, it would. That's
what James 4:4 teaches when it asks this good question:

131

"You adulteresses, do you not know that friendship with the world is hostility toward God?"

## The Enemy of God

God's enemy in this verse is clearly the world. But in what sense is that true?

### The Meaning of the World

When the New Testament speaks of *the world,* it could mean one of three things. First, sometimes the term signifies the physical earth. Acts 17:24 speaks of "the God who made the world and all things in it." But that is not the idea found in James 4:4. It is no sin to love flowers, trees, mountains, and rivers. The physical world of nature is part of the bounty God has given us to enjoy.

Second, *the world* often stands for the people who live in it. John 3:16 is a case in point: "For God so loved the world, that He gave His only begotten Son, that whoever believes in Him should not perish, but have eternal life." Here again, you do not sin when you befriend people. Instead, you follow the example of our heavenly Father. Jesus himself was known as "a friend of . . . sinners" (Matt. 11:19). So James 4:4 cannot have the people of the world in mind when it says that "friendship with the world is hostility toward God."

The term *world* in this verse signifies the customs, habits, and attitude of the world, all of which leave no room for God. Your enemy is everything in the world that is opposed to your Lord and his ways. J. I. Packer says that the world is "the spirit which substitutes some earthly ideal, such as pleasure, or gain, or popularity, for life's true goal, which is in all things to praise and to glorify God" (*God's Words,* [Downers Grove, Ill.: InterVarsity Press], pp.

63–64). Centuries ago John Wesley defined the world as "whatever cools my affection toward Christ." In one word, we can say that what James 4:4 and other similar verses have in mind is *worldliness*.

### The Makeup of the World

A good parallel to James 4:4 is 1 John 2:16. It teaches that "the lust of the flesh and the lust of the eyes and the boastful pride of life" are "all that is in the world." Only three things. Let's look at them one at a time.

#### A Preoccupation with Pleasure

The first ingredient in worldliness is "the lust of the flesh." I know a young man who boasted that he paid to see the same movie more than seventy-five times. Regardless of that movie's title or rating, his behavior was worldly. An undue emphasis on eating and drinking, an inability to control your time in front of the television set or the programs you watch on it, a love for money, or an inordinate craving for clothes all qualify as the lust of the flesh or a preoccupation with pleasure.

#### A Preoccupation with Possessions

The second element in the world is "the lust of the eyes." It occurs when you see something that belongs to someone else and lust to possess it yourself. The tenth commandment warns, "You shall not covet . . . anything that belongs to your neighbor" (Exod. 20:17).

Eve took one look at the forbidden fruit in the Garden of Eden and lusted after it. In the seventh chapter of Joshua, a man named Achan seized some of the spoils from the battle of Jericho. He knew God had placed a ban on them, but when he laid his eyes on the silver, a bar of gold, and a beautiful garment, he snatched them up. When King Ahab saw Naboth's vineyard, his wife Jezebel masterminded

Naboth's murder so the land could be Ahab's. To get his hands on thirty pieces of silver, Judas betrayed Jesus. All of these are examples of "the lust of the eyes," a craving to possess what we see.

Every time a gambler walks into a casino and sees the tables and slot machines, he practices the lust of the eyes. But even in your own home you can commit this sin simply by turning the pages of a mail-order shopping catalog and saying, "I want this and that and that."

In my first pastorate out of seminary I lived in a studio apartment. "Studio" means there was no bedroom, so I had to sleep in the living room. The apartment was also right next to the railroad tracks, and all night long the trains screamed by and shook the building. To say the least, that apartment left a lot to be desired.

Then God moved me to another church, and in the new city I purchased a home with three bedrooms and two bathrooms in a quiet neighborhood. What a change! I was so pleased with my home that for the first time in my life I became house oriented. I found myself driving down the street and envying the beautiful homes other people owned. They were always bigger and better than mine. One day it occurred to me that I was committing "the lust of the eyes." And even after recognizing this problem, the temptation is still there.

### A Preoccupation with Power

The third and final ingredient in the world is "the boastful pride of life." History is studded with examples of famous people who displayed "the boastful pride of life." If George Washington had had his way, he would have been addressed as "His Mightiness, the President of the United States." Christopher Columbus begged for the title "Admiral of the Ocean and Viceroy of India." Catherine the

Great refused to open letters that were not addressed to "Her Imperial Majesty." I suppose she was the one who also saw to it that history remembered her as "The Great." In the White House Abraham Lincoln's wife once turned on Mrs. Grant, the vice president's wife, and shouted, "How dare you be seated in my presence until I invite you!" (Cited by Dale Carnegie, *How to Win Friends and Influence People* [New York: Simon and Schuster, 1952], 31–32).

Let's face it. All of us are confronted every day with the temptation to seize power. What's the cure for this boastful pride of life? A. W. Tozer spells it out in his classic work, *The Pursuit of God:* "Self is the opaque veil that hides the Face of God from us. It can be removed only in a spiritual experience, never by mere instruction. As well try to instruct leprosy out of our system. There must be a work of God in destruction before we are free. We must invite the cross to do its deadly work within us" (A. W. Tozer, *The Pursuit of God* [Harrisburg, Penn.: Christian Publications, Inc., n.d.], 46).

That is the secret we are so slow to learn. We try to free ourselves from the grip of pride, but it never works. We must go to Calvary by faith and see ourselves crucified with Christ. Only then will we gain deliverance from the boastful pride of life.

The crafty thing about worldliness, whether it be a preoccupation with pleasure, possessions, or power, is that it takes place in your heart, where no one can see it. You don't have to *do* anything to be guilty of courting friendship with God's enemy, worldliness. Rather, it's a matter of what you *are*.

## The Enmity toward God

I think it significant that our text, James 4:4, does not say, "Friendship with the world is being hostile toward

God." No, it is *hostility* personified. You not only hate God when you befriend his enemy, you become hatred itself.

### The Inevitability of Enmity

It's no use attempting to excuse your worldly heart on the basis that you don't mean to wage war against God. Worldliness makes it inevitable. Jesus declared in Matthew 6:24 that "no one can serve two masters." A master is someone who demands total obedience and love.

And that's just what God's enemy, the world, is after. Its goal is to usurp the authority of Christ himself. You cannot be worldly and godly at the same time, any more than you can be in the United States and Europe simultaneously. Consequently, it's unavoidable that if you are a friend of the world you are an enemy of God.

Someone may say, "I thought the devil was God's enemy." He is. But three times Jesus called Satan "the ruler of this world" (John 12:31; 14:30; 16:11). And 1 John 5:19 tells us that "the whole world lies in the power of the evil one." Because the world is Satan's friend it is God's enemy. Accept it as a spiritual law, therefore, that if you are a friend of this world—if you are a worldly person—you are an enemy of the heavenly Father.

### The Injury of Enmity

Worldliness promises to bring you joy and fulfillment. But in the end all you have to show for it are scars and a broken heart. The world does not treat its friends kindly. When you become an enemy of God you only injure yourself. Chasing after the world is like running after a butterfly. It looks pretty, but as soon as you grasp it, it crumbles and becomes useless. People who pursue worldliness have nothing to show for their efforts. As C. S. Lewis once said,

"Aim at heaven, and you will get earth thrown in. Aim at earth, and you will get neither."

A ship is made to be in the water. But if the water gets into the ship, watch out! And so with you and the world. You are harmed not by living in the world but by the world living in you. Jesus told you to be *in* the world, so you can bear witness *to* it, but not to be *like* it.

James goes on to say in our text (4:4): "Whoever wishes to be a friend of the world makes himself an enemy of God." The key word is *wishes*. It is a desire to be worldly that ruins people, not a circumstance dictated by environment. You may work in a worldly atmosphere or attend a secular university, but that does not make you God's enemy. On the other hand, it's possible to work in a church and have your heart in the world. Every day you may be surrounded by spiritual people, the office you work in pipes in Christian music, but if you wish to be in the world, you are worldly, and that attitude will always drive a wedge between you and Jesus Christ.

### The Injustice of Enmity

The word translated "hostility" means a "deep-rooted hatred, irreconcilable hostility" (*Unger's Bible Dictionary*). Is that any way to treat the Lord? Does he deserve that? Is it right for you to hate God after he loved you enough to die on the cross for your sins?

Notice how James 4:4 begins by calling us adulteresses. That implies we are Christ's bride, which is exactly what Revelation 19:7 calls us. We thought we were only being friendly with the world, but it seduced us, and as a result we committed adultery against Jesus. In our text James uses the plural, *adulteresses,* to emphasize that every Christian has been unfaithful to Christ. We have all broken our marriage vows to our heavenly bridegroom.

William Barclay has an insightful comment on this word *adulteresses*. He writes: "It means that all sin is a sin against love. It means that our relationship to God is not like the distant relationship of king and subject, or master and slave, but that it is like the intimate relationship of husband and wife. It means that sin is infidelity to love, and that when we sin we break God's heart, as the heart of one partner in a marriage is broken when the other callously and deliberately deserts him or her" (*The Letters of James and Peter* [Edinburgh: St. Andrew Press, 1970], Vol. 14, 120).

Do you think Christ deserves that kind of treatment from you? Is it fair? Surely it is the height of injustice. No loving husband can remain unmoved by the unfaithfulness of his wife. And neither can your heavenly bridegroom. His broken heart over your love for the world proves you have treated him unfairly.

## Personal Application

This good question from James 4:4 serves as a reminder that a worldly heart is a spiritual cancer. You don't even have to fall in love with the world to make yourself an enemy of Jesus. All you need do is shake hands with it as a friend. That is a declaration of war, not merely against God's truth or God's church or God's Word, but against God himself.

Jesus said, "He who is not with Me is against Me" (Matt. 12:30). On whose side are you? Who is your friend, and who is your enemy? Yes, you must have an enemy, for unless you set yourself against the world as it stands under the rule of Satan, you will never be the friend of God.

I once heard about a fireman who rescued a woman from her burning home in Oklahoma. As he carried her on his shoulder out of the flames, she was screaming, "My baby! My baby! My baby!" The rescuer placed her on the lawn and said, "Which room is your baby in?" The frantic mother pointed to the upstairs window.

Swiftly the hero climbed the ladder and felt around in the child's blazing room. He found the crib, reached into it, and scooped up a little bundle wrapped in a blanket. He escaped from the room seconds before it was engulfed in flames. As he started down the ladder, the onlookers cheered. They could see the baby blanket under his strong arm. When he touched the ground, the mother was anxiously waiting. She snatched the bundle from him, unwrapped the blanket, and began wailing. Then she screamed, "You picked up my baby's *doll,* not my baby!"

The anguish that fireman felt will be shared by many people when they stand before Jesus on the judgment day. They will be found clutching the toys and trinkets of this world that they considered precious and on which they staked their lives. What they thought was their greatest friend will turn out to be God's enemy. And it will betray them into eternal judgment.

Perhaps you have genuinely trusted Jesus as your personal Savior and have been delivered from judgment. But just as a bride can cheat on her husband, so bona fide believers can prove to be adulteresses in relation to Christ. If the world with all its empty promises has seduced you, it's time for a recommitment of yourself to the Lord, isn't it?

Friendship with the world will make you an enemy of Christ. But with Jesus you don't have to settle for mere friendship. You can be his loving bride, bearing no trace of any sinful spot, wrinkle, or blemish. I wouldn't want to forfeit that for all the world. Would you?

# 14

# A Question of Calling

"Whom shall I send, and who will go for Us?"
(Isa. 6:8)

In the year 740 B.C. the prophet Isaiah heard God ask a question that was to alter the course of his life. It is found in Isaiah 6:8: "Whom shall I send, and who will go for Us?" Note the individuality, "Whom shall I send?" and the plurality, "Who will go for Us?" Here is an Old Testament hint of the Trinity. The three persons of the Godhead are one in their purpose. The Father, Son, and Holy Spirit are united in their desire to dispatch witnesses to the remotest parts of the world so that people may hear the gospel and find salvation in Christ.

In this great text God speaks not just to Isaiah but to you and me. He wants to send us out to share the good news of Jesus Christ with people who desperately need to hear it.

141

## The Call God Extends to Us

Perhaps for years you've been praying that your husband, wife, or friend would trust Christ. But you've seen no results. You're tempted to wonder if God even cares. Rest assured he does—far more than you or I do. First Timothy 2:3–4 speaks of "God our Savior, who desires all men to be saved and to come to the knowledge of the truth." In 2 Peter 3:9 we learn that "the Lord is not . . . wishing for any to perish but for all to come to repentance." God yearns for the salvation of mankind so much that he sent his only Son to Calvary's cross to pay the penalty for the sins of the world. That's why he cries out to us who know him, "Who will go for Us?"

I believe you can hear the heavenly voice saying to you, "Whom shall I send, and who will go for Us?" in circumstantial ways. God speaks through the despairing cries of battered wives, abused children, and the terminally ill. He speaks through the African native who sings to his star gods. When the arrogant, sophisticated atheist proclaims, "There is no God," you can translate that into heaven's language as, "Who will go for Us?" The challenge of the nonbeliever to the Lord is the Lord's challenge to the believer. The very sins of people evoke the heavenly Father's voice, calling you and me to witness to them.

Near the end of the eighteenth century in Northampton, England, a young man named William Carey expressed his sense of divine call to the mission field. He was attending a pastors' meeting at the time. The moderator, John Ryland, pounded his gavel and shouted at Carey, "Young man, sit down! When God is pleased to convert the heathen, he will do it without your help or mine." But William Carey refused to sit down while people were perishing. He was soon off to India, and today he is known as the father of modern missions. He heard God's call and obeyed.

Four-year-old Hudson Taylor would tell visitors in his home, "When I grow up, I'm going to be a missionary to China." Years later, while sailing to China, he was questioned by the ship's captain: "Taylor, do you mean to tell me that the heathen will be lost if you don't go to China?"

"I believe the heathen are *already* lost," the man of God replied, "and that's why I'm going to China." He had responded to God's question, "Who will go for Us?"

Jim Elliot was a missionary martyred by the Auca Indians on January 8, 1956. During his college years he spent a summer as a missionary intern on an Indian reservation. There he wrote in his journal: "Glad to get the opportunity to preach the Gospel of the matchless grace of our God to stoical, pagan Indians. I only hope that He will let me preach to those who have never heard that name Jesus. What else is worthwhile in this life? I have heard of nothing better. Lord, send me." (Elisabeth Elliot, *Through Gates of Splendor* [New York: Harper & Row, 1957], 18).

In 1856 James Chalmers, then fifteen years old, heard God's call and vowed to take the good news of Christ to cannibals. He later traveled to New Guinea. There he was clubbed to death, beheaded, and eaten by men whom he had loved and to whom he had preached the gospel. He gladly gave his life, because he had heard God say, "Who will go for Us?"

Have you heard those words? If you do not witness to your family, your neighbors, your co-workers, or your friends, who will? And who will span the globe as missionaries if all God's children leave that responsibility to someone else? Don't think your pastor can do your work for you. He has spiritual labors of his own to keep him busy. The Lord has placed you in your sphere of influence as his messenger to people who might otherwise not know Jesus Christ.

God wants every Christian to be involved in evangelism. You are saved to serve. Why, then, are so many uninvolved? Perhaps because there is a missing link between God's call and their qualifications. The volunteer spirit by itself isn't enough. To be the Lord's instruments of change in other people's lives, you must possess specific characteristics.

## The Characteristics God Expects of Us

The context of Isaiah 6:8 is a thumbnail sketch of five characteristics of the person whom God can use.

### Conviction

Conviction is a shattering realization that sin has defiled you and rendered you helpless to do anything about it. Notice Isaiah's personal testimony in the opening of verse 5: "Then I said, 'Woe is me, for I am ruined!'" The King James Version uses the word *undone* at the end of that sentence. A few verses earlier the prophet tells that he witnessed a vision of the Lord in his holiness. When he saw that, Isaiah came unraveled. His peers would have said he had it all together. But he sensed that he was falling apart at the seams. His reputation as a righteous man melted like a snowflake in an oven while he was in the presence of the Lord of glory. He was "undone."

Have you ever felt like that? Have you ever come unraveled at the thought that apart from Christ you are a guilty and condemned sinner? Can you say with Isaiah, "Woe is me, for I am undone"?

Only when you understand your nothingness can Christ fill you. As long as you suppose you can offer God your good works, talents, or abilities, all your labors for him will be performed in the strength of sinful flesh. And that never accomplishes anything spiritual or eternal. In his autobiography Charles Spurgeon tells of his own experience of conviction: "Before I thought upon my soul's salvation, I dreamed that my sins were very few. All my sins were dead, as I imagined, and buried in the graveyard of forgetfulness. But that trumpet of conviction, which aroused my soul to think of eternal things, sounded a resurrection-note to all my sins; and, oh, how they rose up in multitudes more countless than the sands of the sea! Now, I saw that my very thoughts were enough to damn me, that my words would sink me lower than the lowest hell, and as for my acts of sin, they now began to be a stench in my nostrils so that I could not bear them" (C. H. Spurgeon: *Autobiography,* [Edinburgh: The Banner of Truth Trust, 1976], Vol. 1, *The Early Years*: 59). No wonder Spurgeon went on to become the "prince of preachers." God had healed him of a mortal heart wound.

### Confession

In the next line of verse 5 Isaiah admits, "I am a man of unclean lips." The Living Bible puts it like this: "I am a foul-mouthed sinner." Was profanity Isaiah's besetting sin? Some commentators think so. Or perhaps he is confessing acts of lying, slander, or gossip.

In any case, the prophet is specific in his confession. He knows the Lord is confronting him with his spiritually unclean speech. It's easy to say, "Yes, I'm a sinner," but much more difficult to confess, "I'm a liar," or "I'm addicted to alcohol," or "I'm enslaved to lust." What is your besetting sin? Do you tend to pray, "Lord, forgive me for all my sins"? That's better than nothing, but the core of confession is an exposure of specific crimes against a holy God.

Sometimes we entangle ourselves in counterfeit confessions. We may tell a spouse, "I'm sorry I was selfish and unloving. But you'll have to accept me as I am." Or we try to blame someone else for our sins. "Lord forgive me for my anger," someone says, "but if my children hadn't provoked me, I wouldn't have lost control." That's not coming to grips with sin. As long as we use such cop-outs, God cannot forgive us.

If Isaiah could admit that he was a man of unclean lips, can't we own up to our sins? As a spokesman for God, the worst problem Isaiah could have had was unclean, sinful lips. Imagine a school teacher who can't read or an airline pilot who is afraid of heights. That's how Isaiah felt as a prophet with unclean lips. He was confessing his total unworthiness to fulfill God's calling. And when we come to that same admission of unworthiness, our Lord will receive all the glory for any spiritual fruit in our lives.

### Concern

In verse 5 Isaiah goes on to say: "And I live among a people of unclean lips." The prophet cared that his countrymen were far from the Lord. He grieved over their impure speech, because it was a telltale sign of their corrupt hearts. As Jesus would later say: "The mouth speaks out of that which fills the heart" (Matt. 12:34).

Once a pastor named Burns stood on a crowded street corner in Glasgow, Scotland, with tears streaming down his cheeks. When questioned about his tears, he replied, "The thud of Christless feet on the road to hell is breaking my heart." He was concerned for his people who had unclean, sinful lips and lives.

Does it make any difference to you that people are breaking God's laws as thoughtlessly as a child breaks crackers into crumbs? Does it matter to you that some of your friends, neighbors, and perhaps even family members are a heartbeat away from hell? Are you concerned about the sin your children want to watch on your television set? Without a heartfelt sorrow on your part you are unusable to God.

### Conversion

In verses 6 and 7 we read of Isaiah's conversion: "Then one of the seraphim flew to me, with a burning coal in his hand which he had taken from the altar with tongs. And he touched my mouth with it and said, 'Behold, this has touched your lips; and your iniquity is taken away, and your sin is forgiven.'" Note that Isaiah's conversion in verses 6 and 7 precedes his call to ministry in verse 8.

I believe this is where many churches reveal a blind spot. They allow nonbelievers to exercise a ministry. God's work should be carried out by God's children. I refer not merely to preaching and teaching. Enlisting non-Christians as ushers, choir members, or nursery workers turns these ministries into bare programs at best and hypocritical shams at worst. God wants his work carried out by loving servants, not rebels. Even Isaiah was not called until he was converted.

But mark this. He was called on the same day he was converted. Maybe you haven't trusted Christ yet. But if you give him your heart now, he will put you to work right away. Often brand-new believers make the best witnesses for Christ.

### Consecration

When the Lord asked, "Whom shall I send, and who will go for Us?" Isaiah answered, "Here am I. Send me!" He did not plead, "Send someone else, anyone but me." He had just seen a vision of angels, but he did not say, "There are the seraphim. Send them." He did not beg the question by answering, "Here is my tithe, send it to support missionaries." Nor did he dodge his duty by replying, "Here is my son. I dedicate him to your service. Send him." No. Isaiah was personally consecrated to God. He answered, "Here am I. Send *me*!"

Isaiah was willing to go for God. Are you? I know a woman who prayed that the Lord would call people into missionary service. But when her own son announced that he was called, she panicked and tried to hold him back. I heard another woman beg God in prayer for months to convert her husband. Her request was granted. But she became bitter when her husband also obeyed the Lord's call into the pastoral ministry. She even confessed, "That was more than I bargained for."

I think it significant that Isaiah did not say, "Here am I. Use me right here." He was willing to be sent. He didn't know where the Lord would dispatch him, but wherever it was, he would go. He offered himself unreservedly to God. Nor did Isaiah presumptuously run off to do his own thing and say that it was the Lord's work. He waited to be sent by the divine hand.

Right now you may be thinking, "What could I ever do for Christ?" You could do what he asks. Someone once said, "I am only one person, but I am one. I cannot do everything, but I can do something. What I can do, I ought to do, and what I ought to do, by the grace of God I will do."

You may protest, "I'm too young to serve the Lord." Jeremiah made that excuse, and it got him nowhere. Instead say, "Lord, I'm young, but I give you my youthful life. Here am I. Send me!" If you are elderly, say, "Father, I don't have much time left, but what I have is all yours. Here am I. Send me!" If you are poor, tell the Lord, "Silver and gold have I none, but what I have I give to you. Send me!" If you are rich, lay your wealth on the altar and say,

"Father, you've loaned me everything I have. Send me and my money into your service." If God has given you a beautiful singing voice, a sharp mind, a compassionate heart, or anything else that can bring him glory, consecrate it to him by praying, "Here am I. Send me!"

## Personal Application

Still today our triune God asks, "Who will go for us?" Where does he want you to go? It could be to the other side of the world as a missionary, across the street to witness to your non-Christian neighbors, or into your children's bedrooms to read the Bible, share Christ's love, and pray with them. Will you go for God? Are you willing to say with Isaiah, "Here am I. Send me"?

In 1868 Daniel March was invited to preach to the Christian Association in Philadelphia. He felt led to speak on the twofold question of Isaiah 6:8: "Whom shall I send, and who will go for Us?" But the day before he was to preach he learned that the hymn selected for the close of the service touched on some other topic. So that night, full of his subject, he composed a hymn based on this text. It is the only one by which Daniel March is known as a hymn writer. The following day at the close of his sermon it was sung, and ever since it has stirred the souls of believers. I leave it with you now:

> Hark, the voice of Jesus calling,
> "Who will go and work today?
> Fields are white, and harvests waiting,
> Who will bear the sheaves away?"
> Loud and long the Master calleth,
> Rich reward He offers thee;
> Who will answer, gladly saying,

"Here am I; send me; send me"?

If you cannot cross the ocean
And the heathen lands explore,
You can find the heathen nearer,
You can help them at your door.
If you cannot give your thousands,
You can give the widow's mite;
And the least you give for Jesus
Will be precious in His sight.

Let none hear you idly saying,
"There is nothing I can do,"
While the souls of men are dying,
And the Master calls for you.
Gladly take the task He gives you;
Let His work your pleasure be;
Answer quickly when He calleth,
"Here am I. Send me! Send me!"

—Daniel March, 1868

# 15

# A Question of Difficulty

"Is anything too difficult for Me?" (Jer. 32:27)

Some time ago a woman came to my office deeply troubled over her husband. He said he still loved her and was not leaving her for another woman. But he seemed hopelessly in bondage to alcohol. From the depths of depression this woman related to me her misery in marriage. She contemplated divorcing her husband in an attempt to find peace and happiness. I inquired into her spiritual life and learned that she had already placed her faith in Christ as her personal Savior.

"Do you believe that God can change your husband?" I asked.

She looked me in the eye and after a period of silence answered, "No, I don't."

I pointed the woman to Jeremiah 32:27, which reads: "Behold, I am the LORD, the God of all flesh; is anything too difficult for Me?" This is a question that nags even at the hearts of Christians. We struggle with it, so let's consider it in three ways.

## The Answer to the Question

We know, at least theologically, that nothing is too difficult for God. But skeptics have often asked, "Could God make a rock so heavy that even he couldn't lift it?" Either way you answer that question you feel you deny his omnipotence. But the Bible is not embarrassed to admit that there are some things the Lord cannot do. Hebrews 6:18 says: "It is impossible for God to lie." James 1:13 tells us he "cannot be tempted by evil." And 2 Timothy 2:13 states that "He cannot deny Himself."

These passages do not divest God of his omnipotence; they teach that he is only limited by his own perfections. Because he is perfect, he cannot lie, be tempted by evil, or deny himself. No good thing is too difficult for our Lord, and no evil thing is too strong to overpower him. That's omnipotence.

God appeared to Sarah when she was ninety years old and told her she was going to have a baby. The thought was so ridiculous to her that she laughed. Then God rebuked her with the same question he asked Jeremiah: "Is anything too difficult for the LORD?" (Gen. 18:14). Sure enough, a year later she gave birth to a son, whom she named Isaac, which in Hebrew means "Laughter." Every time Sarah called his name, she reminded herself of the day she laughed in God's face at the thought of an impossible situation.

A few years later the Lord told Sarah's husband, Abraham,

to offer Isaac on the altar of sacrifice. Abraham obeyed without question. God even had to stop him at the last instant before he plunged his knife into Isaac's throat. When the Lord saw Abraham's willingness to obey, it was enough.

Do you know why Abraham was so ready to sacrifice his son? Hebrews 11:19 tells us: "He considered that God is able to raise men even from the dead." At that point in history no one had ever come back from the dead. But Abraham knew that not even a resurrection was too difficult for the Lord, and he was willing to obey the divine command to prove it.

When Joshua led the army of Israel to victory over the Amorites, darkness approached before his job was completed. So he asked the Lord to make the sun stand still so he could finish the job. (We might say he wanted to beat the daylights out of the Amorites.) Was it a foolish prayer request? That depends. Do you believe that halting the rotation of the earth is too difficult for God? And is it too hard a job for him to overrule all the side effects of this miracle?

Or, look at Jesus. He enters Bethany where his friend Lazarus has been dead four days. The first thing he hears from both of the grieving sisters is, "Lord, if You had been here, my brother would not have died" (John 11:21,32). Does Jesus apologize for being absent when Lazarus was sick? No! He raises him from the dead, graveclothes and all. Nothing is too difficult for Jesus Christ.

In his poem, "Convinced," Strickland W. Gillilan expresses the struggle of every Christian to believe in God's power.

> I have listened to agnostics since my childhood days of faith,
> Till the trust my mother taught me seemed as fleetin' as a wraith;

I have shed the light of reason on the Bible tales, and
     thought
That the miracles it told about could never have been
     wrought.
I have proved beyond a question that such doin's hadn't
     been—
But when I sit and read my Bible, I believe 'em all agin.

I have heard it proved by science that the sun-delayin'
     stunt
That is credited to Joshua's an error; you may hunt
Through the volumes of biology from frontispiece to end
For the fish that swallowed Jonah, but she isn't there, my
     friend.
That the masonry of Jericho should tumble at the toot
Of a lot of sheepish headgear is a tale at which they hoot.
But although the things I mention seem preposterously
     thin,
When I sit and read 'em over, I believe 'em all agin.

Take the one about where Samson with the jawbone of a
     mule
Tackled thousands of Philistines with this funny fightin'
     tool;
That there tale of Neb'chadnezzar going grazing like a
     steer,
Would impress the careless hearer as at least a trifle
     queer;
While that one about the donkey rode by Balaam
     speaking out,
That one's quite as hard a story to believe—or just about.
To be brief, there's lots of stories with a world of
     queerness in,
But when reading in my Bible, I believe 'em all agin.

It's not a matter of conjecture, it's a certainty, you see,
Wonderfuller things have happened to such dubs as you
     and me;

There's our mothers still a loving us through all these
    fruitless years—
Yes, I'll stop it if you think that I am tapping you for
    tears.
Nature's doing things each minute with a lot more
    wonders in,
So I sit and read my Bible and believe it all agin.

Can you say that? Have you settled in your heart the
question of God's ability? Is there anything you can think
of that is too difficult for him?

"Like what?" you ask. Let me make some suggestions in
our next heading.

## The Application of the Question

Sometimes our doubt centers around our own sinfulness
of heart. A man told me that he had ruined so many people
through his vile influence that he considered himself
unpardonable.

Often such a claim is a camouflage hiding an unwilling-
ness to repent. But some people do have serious problems
accepting divine forgiveness. Even Isaac Watts wrote in his
hymn:

Alas! and did my Savior bleed?
And did my Sovereign die?
Would He devote that sacred head
For such a worm as I?

I believe we are spiritual worms. Sin makes us disgusting
in God's eyes, and that's a hindrance to the faith of some.
However, it's not the *hindrance* to faith but the *object* of
faith that counts. Take your eyes off your sins and put
them on Christ. The wonder of his love is that he knew

perfectly well how depraved you and I would be, yet he died for us anyway. Make no mistake; it takes every drop of omnipotence to forgive one sinner. The most amazing feat of power the world has ever seen was accomplished on the cross when Jesus won salvation for sinners. And that proves that nothing is beyond the reach of God's strength.

Surely you yearn for non-Christian family members and friends to trust Christ. You witness to them, share the gospel with them, pray for them, and love them. But they remain unmoved. Sometimes you may feel that God is at the mercy of their unbelief, that he wants to save them but is hindered by their stubbornness. You know your heavenly Father speaks to his children but wonder if even he can get through to nonbelievers who seem unreachable.

Look again at Jeremiah 32:27: "Behold, I am the LORD, the God of all flesh." Those last two words are translated "all mankind" in the New International Version. So our Lord can pierce hearts that are petrified against him. When God sovereignly decides to make someone a Christian there's no resisting him. This is not to say that he forces us to believe against our will. Instead, he makes us willing. He opens our eyes to the truth, and immediately we fall in love with Christ. If our Lord should give the order, that godless husband of yours would fall to the ground, confess his sins in humble repentance, and surrender his heart to Christ. Nothing is too difficult for the God of all mankind.

Temptation is another area in which you may doubt your Lord's might. You easily yield to various enticements because even as a Christian you feel helpless against them. As a result, you become an easy mark for the fiery missiles of your enemy, the devil.

Don't confuse the Lord's power with your own. You know you are no match for temptation, so you assume your heavenly Father isn't, either. But think again. Is God able to liberate you from drug addiction, alcoholism, smoking, lust, profanity, temper tantrums, pride, and jealousy, or isn't he? Perhaps you feel that if the Lord could set you free from your secret sins it would be the greatest miracle in the world. Then hear him say, "Behold, I am the LORD, the God of all flesh; is anything too difficult for Me?"

Maybe you've given up hope of seeing your broken marriage restored. A woman I'll call Jean told me that her daughter's marriage was on the brink of failure. Though Debbie and Steve were once the perfect Christian couple, Steve no longer felt any love for her. He became a different man. Every day he screamed at Debbie, cursed her, and told her to move out. He was unwilling to seek counseling and had also stopped attending church. One day without warning Debbie came home from work to discover that Steve had moved out.

Jean had faith that God would restore love in Steve's heart for her daughter. So she encouraged Debbie to wait on the Lord. But Debbie's father, whom I'll call David, kept telling her to face facts, that the marriage was over, and she should file for divorce. Jean confronted David about that and said, "You're leaving God out of this."

Quickly David replied, "Even God can't keep this marriage together."

Jean looked her husband in the eye and said, "If he could rebuild our marriage, he can rebuild Steve and Debbie's." David was silenced.

Debbie's hopes had been reduced to nothing—except God. My wife and I joined her and many other Christians in fervent prayer for Steve. Humanly speaking he was hopelessly resolved to have his own way. But four months later he came under the Holy Spirit's conviction. For several weeks he tried to resist it but finally confessed his sin to God and to Debbie, with whom he also sought reconciliation.

Soon after moving back into the family home, Steve announced at the dinner table to their two children, "I'm going to spend the rest of my life making your mother happy." Incredible words! Hearing of them later, I could hardly believe they came from the same mouth that a few months earlier had been spewing curses. The reconciliation of Steve and Debbie served as a vivid reminder to me and many others that nothing is too difficult for our Lord.

There are many other areas in which we could apply the question God asks in our text. Is it too hard a task for the Lord to straighten out your wayward children? Can he heal you of a terminal disease? Will he answer your prayers? Can he find you the right job? Yes, he can do all these things. He is the Lord, and nothing is too difficult for him.

## The Admonitions from the Question

This good question admonishes us in at least two ways. First, it urges us to seize our seemingly hopeless situations as wonderful opportunities to trust our Lord. Years ago a friend and I were driving to an important meeting. But we were late, so we took a shortcut off the highway onto a deserted, unpaved road. It had recently rained, and the wheels of my car became caught in the mud. The endless spinning of the tires wound up my frustration. My friend turned to me and said, "Tom, isn't this a great opportunity the Lord is giving us to trust him to get us out of this mess?" That question stung my heart, for I had given up all hope of arriving at our appointment on time.

Soon a stranger drove up and pulled us out with a chain. Then the Lord rebuked me for worrying when I should have been trusting. I was reminded that nothing is too difficult for God.

Don't we tend to take our daily trials, like mine with the car stuck in the mud, as our biggest tests of faith? Surely God is worthy of our trust in our everyday problems, just as he is in that once-in-a-lifetime crisis. Nothing is too difficult for him.

Second, Jeremiah 32:27 encourages us to act on our faith. It's easy to believe in the doctrine of God's omnipotence. But when an impossible situation confronts us, can we cease worrying and trust our Lord to see us through?

John and Hilda Williams are precious friends of mine. Once, while teaching a Bible class, John encouraged his students to claim the promises of Scripture as if they were collecting on an insurance policy. Not many days later John and Hilda received news that their only son, who was thirty-five, had died of a heart attack. The jaws of grief overwhelmed them. But in the middle of the night John awoke with this thought: "Now is the time to collect on our spiritual insurance. This is when we have to cash in on our Christian faith." He shared the insight with his wife, and together they agreed to accept Christ's offer of help and strength.

The next day they traveled to their son's home to pick up his possessions. Their peace was so great that they even slept in his room. God used both of them to encourage many others who were being tested in crucibles of their own. John and Hilda proved in their furnace of affliction that it wasn't too difficult for God to sustain them in their sorrow and turn their tragedy into triumph.

## Personal Application

What is your impossible situation? What is the most difficult thing in life you need God to accomplish for you? I think a good follow-up question to this one in Jeremiah 32:27 would be, "Is it too difficult for *you* to trust in an almighty God?" The real weakness lies not in your Father but in your faith. I close with a poem by Sarah Bess Geibel that beautifully summarizes Jeremiah 32:27:

Who of us doesn't wonder in moments of despair,
"Is anything too hard for God, and does He really care?"
The God of grace is also God of every crisis too;
No circumstance can be too hard for Him to see us
    through.

When we pass through waters safely or through the fire
    unburned,
Against the backdrop of despair, His presence is
    discerned.
For God to clothe Himself in flesh and suffer for our
    loss,
Ah, nothing was too hard for Him—not even the cruel
    cross.

I see by faith with tear-dimmed eyes His bleeding thorn-
    crowned head,
Five wounds in hands and feet and side I should have
    had instead.
Is anything too hard for God, the whole or even the
    part?
O God who always does what's best, forgive my doubt-
    prone heart.

No, nothing is too hard for Thee; forgive my unbelief.
With Thomas and all saints, O Christ, I fall at Thy dear
    feet!